J. M. Longridge
January 27th, 1995.

The British Library gratefully acknowledges the financial support of
Shell Switzerland in making the production of this book possible.

S W I T Z E R L A N D ✚ 700

Peter Barber

and curators of the British Library and the British Museum

© 1991 The British Library Board

First published 1991 by
The British Library
Great Russell Street
London WC1B 3DG

Publication is made possible by a grant from
Shell Switzerland

All the coins, medals, watches, and all the prints
in Part III.1., are reproduced by permission
of the Trustees of the British Museum.
The maps on page 15 are reproduced by
permission of George Philip & Son Ltd. and
of the Co-ordinating Commission for the
Presence of the Swiss Abroad.

British Library Cataloguing in Publication Data

Switzerland 700: Treasures from the British Library
and British Museum to celebrate 700 years
of the Swiss Confederation.

1. Switzerland
I. Barber, Peter *1948-*   II. British Museum   III. British Library
949.4

ISBN 0 7123 0258 1 (cased)
ISBN 0 7123 0257 3 (paperback)

Designed by Terry Anthony, Shell International
Printed in Great Britain by BPCC Hazell Books, Paulton

Foreword

The Festival of Switzerland is a year-long opportunity to celebrate seven hundred years of the Swiss Confederation and to promote understanding in the United Kingdom of Switzerland and the Swiss through an extensive and varied programme of events around the country.

As so many of the programmed events demonstrate, the links between Switzerland and the United Kingdom are long-standing and close, firmly established across the whole spectrum of diplomatic, cultural, religious and commercial relations. Very importantly, however, the links have been very personal, reflecting the experiences of individuals in both countries over the centuries. The Festival programme, covering concerts, literature and theatre, cinema, photography, painting, food and wine, will provide a splendid means of extending these links.

This book, associated with the "Switzerland 700" exhibition at the British Library, is a marvellous survey of the history of Switzerland as seen through the eyes of artists, craftsmen, historians, philosophers and travellers. It illustrates not only the story of Switzerland, but also the extent and variety of the links between the United Kingdom and Switzerland down the years. The book will be a highly appropriate and permanent reminder of these links and of the Festival that celebrates them.

The British Library and their patrons, Shell Switzerland, are to be congratulated on creating so excellent a means of reinforcing and increasing awareness of the nature and extent of Anglo-Swiss relations.

His Royal Highness
The Prince of Wales

The President of
The Swiss Confederation

Preface

by Peter Barber

The British Library is proud to participate in the celebrations marking Switzerland's 700th birthday by displaying some of its Swiss and Anglo-Swiss treasures. Most have rarely, if ever, been on exhibition; others are of sufficient importance to be on permanent display. The book is divided into three parts. The first provides a chronological and geographical framework. The second and largest explores several important themes in Swiss history and culture as reflected, predominantly, in the British Library's collections. All the themes are followed through several centuries to the present day, but the first four were particularly significant in different periods: the diversity in the period of greatest growth before 1550, the military and neutrality in the period from 1516 to about 1800, the country as a bastion of liberty in the eighteenth and early nineteenth centuries and tourism from about 1770 to the present day. These considerations have dictated their position in the book. Most of the single items represent a major strand in each theme, as is explained in the text, and several items could easily have been placed in other sections since they in reality illustrate more than one theme. The last part of the book concentrates on Swiss or Swiss-related stamps, prints, coins, medals, clocks and watches from the holdings of the British Museum and the British Library.

Inevitably the selection of items has been subjective and perhaps idiosyncratic. The aim has been to give an impression of the wealth of our Swiss and Anglo-Swiss holdings and to introduce non-Swiss readers to a few important aspects of the history and culture of the peoples of Switzerland. The selection constitutes only the tip of the iceberg of our holdings, and inevitably many important facets have had to be omitted. For instance, as might be expected from one of the greatest libraries in the world, we possess first editions of most of the classics of Swiss literature, but

their relative lack of visual appeal to all but a small minority has led to their exclusion. Any seriously interested potential reader, however, is most welcome to visit our reading rooms if he is unable to study these books elsewhere. They can easily be traced in our catalogues by searching under the author's name. In the automated system that will come into operation in the reading rooms in our new building at St. Pancras from 1993, they will be retrievable under title, parts of title, language, place of publication and numerous other entry points.

My colleagues in the British Museum, of which the Bloomsbury departments of the British Library formed a part until 1973, have also contributed very substantially to the exhibitions on which this book is based. They agreed to two loans to the main exhibition, mounted related displays of their holdings of prints and of coins and medals, and agreed to highlight clocks, watches and other objects that are on permanent display. While collectively this constituted a 'Swiss Trail' throughout the British Museum building during the period of the exhibition, the single, highlighted objects, books and manuscripts have been integrated into the themes explored in the first part of the book.

The exhibition and this book have very much been a collaborative effort and I would like to thank all my fellow-contributors: David Beech (III.4), Benet Bergonzi (II.5.10), Tim Burnett (II.6.11), Richard Christophers (II.4.7), John Goldfinch (II.5.1), Mervyn Jannetta (II.4.1), Graham Nattrass (II.1.10; II.5.8; II.5.11), Denis Reidy (II.1.13; III.4), Arthur Searle (II.3.5) and particularly Teresa Vernon (II.3.2; II.3.3; II.5.7; II.6.1; II.6.5). The sections on prints (III.1), watches (III.2), and coins and medals (III.3) in the last part of the book were contributed by our British Museum colleagues, Paul Goldman (who also contributed II.6.10), John Leopold and

Philip Attwood. Thanks for their willing support are also due to all my colleagues in the Map Library, Manuscripts and Philatelic collections, particularly J. N. Davies; to the British Library exhibition team ably led by Alan Sterenberg; to the designers Terry Anthony of Shell International (book) and David Burrows (exhibition); to the conservators of the British Library and to the British Library photographers Elizabeth Hunter, Andrew Ogilvie and Laurence Pordes; to Marion Archibald, Julia Bartrum, Andrew Burnett, Lucille Burns, John Cherry, Barrie Cook, Virginia Hewitt, Antony Griffiths, Ian Jenkins, Mark Jones, Lindsay Stainton, Neil Stratford, David Thompson, Nicholas Turner and to all the photographers of the British Museum; to David Way of the British Library, and to Larry McMahon of Shell International for their great assistance in the publishing of this book. We are also most grateful to Frank Allegranza and Luigi Bozzini for the loan of the 1924 Unione Ticinese invitation (II.6.12), and to Clare Wright of the National Army Museum for her advice on British-Swiss military matters. Jane Carr, Virgil Berti and Peter Jacomelli had the kindness to read the text in draft. I have tried to follow most of their suggestions.

We would particularly want to thank Albert Mehr, until recently Swiss Consul-General in the United Kingdom, and Samuel Plattner of Swiss Television, without whose encouragement and support in the early stages this book and the exhibition would have remained simply a missed opportunity.

Above all, however, we owe an enormous debt of gratitude to Shell (Switzerland), not only for their unstinting financial support but for the sustained enthusiasm, sympathy and sensitivity towards our objectives of their representatives, and most notably Jorgen Perch-Nielsen, Eric Zanetti and Raffaella Ferrari.

Contents

Arms of Uri by an artist belonging to the
Circle of Daniel Lindtmayer. From G. Della Torre,
Descriptio Helvetiae (1607) [II.2.2]

INTRODUCTION

The British Library, the British Museum and Switzerland

The links between the British Museum, its library (now part of the British Library) and Switzerland go back far earlier than the foundation of the British Museum in 1753. The antiquary, Sir Robert Cotton (1571-1631), whose manuscripts form one of the Museum and now Library's foundation collections, acquired Tudor state papers, which include diplomatic correspondence from and relating to Switzerland from the opening years of the sixteenth century, as well as the scholarly correspondence of English and Swiss scholars and divines dating from the same period. Over the centuries this core has been expanded through the acquisition of the papers of innumerable statesmen, generals and diplomats, including those of such Swiss as Frederic Haldimand, Henri Bouquet and Luke Schaub who served Britain with distinction in these capacities in America and Europe. As a result the British Library's holdings of such political material in Great Britain are rivalled only by those of the Public Record Office.

Sir Hans Sloane, 1745,
by J.A. Dassier.　　*[III.3.114]*

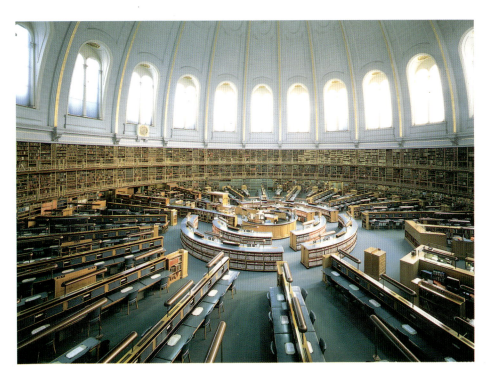

The Round Reading Room in the British Museum, constructed 1852-7.

Human links with Switzerland have also been important. For much of the 1720s Sir Hans Sloane, whose collections formed the basis for the British Museum, employed as his librarian Johann Caspar Scheuchzer (1702-1729), the brilliant but short-lived son of the leading Swiss naturalist Johann Jacob Scheuchzer, whose work is included in this book. It is due to Johann Caspar's judgement that the British Library possesses treasures such as the writings and maps of the German explorer and ethnographer Engelbert Kämpfer, and the Sloane manuscripts also contain some of Scheuchzer's private papers and correspondence. During his own long life, Sloane (1660-1753) was in regular correspondence with the leading Swiss scientists and luminaries of his time and their letters survive in considerable profusion among his papers.

Between 1753 and 1827 the British Museum owed much to the benevolent Swiss influence of the Planta family which had long been established in Castasegna in the Val Bregaglia, Graubünden. The father, Andrew, a protestant clergyman who arrived in England in 1752, served as an Assistant Librarian in the British Museum from 1753 to 1758 before becoming Assistant Keeper of Natural History and finally Assistant Keeper of Printed Books from 1765 until his death in 1773. He was succeeded by his son Joseph (1744-1827) who after 23 years as Keeper of Manuscripts, served as Principal Librarian and, in effect, Director of the British Museum, from 1799 until 1827. Apart from compiling

Joseph Planta
Reproduced by courtesy
of the Trustees of
The British Museum

The 'Escalade':
Savoyard troops attacking Geneva by night,
1602. From the autograph album of
Joachim Camerarius, 1625. *Egerton MS 3039, f.73*

or supervising the compilation of several scholarly catalogues, he gave the Museum the administrative structure that it preserved in its essentials until 1973. More importantly, he liberalised the admissions procedures, improved conditions for readers and finally, in 1814, confirmed for all time the British Museum's legal right to a copy of every book published in the United Kingdom: some of the most important legacies of the British Museum and of the British Library of today. Nor did Joseph Planta forget his homeland and, in addition to scholarly articles on Romansch, he also published a two volume *History of the Helvetic Confederacy* in 1800 and in 1807 a supplementary *View of the Restoration of the Helvetic Confederacy*. More recently the department of Western Asiatic Antiquities of the British Museum had a Swiss keeper in the person of Edmond Sollberger until a few years ago.

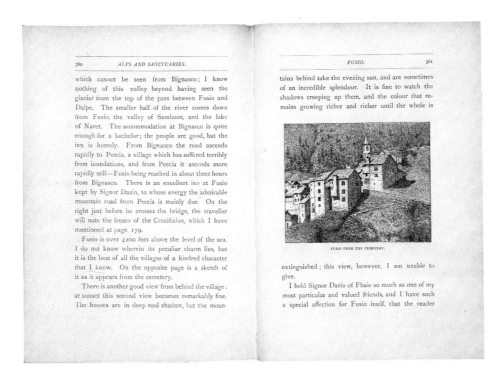

It is in the field of its holdings, however, that links between the British Library and British Museum and Switzerland are strongest. Many departments of the Museum and every section of the Library in Bloomsbury has collections with a significant Swiss element, quite apart from outstanding single items, such as the Moutier Grandval Bible, the della Torre *Descriptio Helvetiae* or an early (1625) miniature painting in an autograph album depicting the attempt of the Duke of Savoy to seize Geneva by stealth in 1602. Thus the British Library is enriched by the large collections of eighteenth century drawings and watercolours by Samuel Hieronymus Grimm and by John Webber who accompanied Cook on his last voyage. It has large numbers of rare early sixteenth century pamphlets, often adorned with fine woodcuts, published particularly in Basle and Zurich and relating to theological and political developments of the time. The collections bequeathed by Thomas Sydney Blakeney (1903-76), an enthusiastic mountaineer, are rich in manuscripts and rare printed material relating to England and the Alps. The British Library's part of the papers of Samuel Butler, which are divided between several libraries, also contains many letters written by and to him from southern Switzerland at the end of the last century, amplifying the account given of the area in *Alps and Sanctuaries*. In the Tapling Collection the Library possesses valuable holdings of early Swiss stamps including unique sets of cantonal issues from Zurich.

The collection of superlative watercolours and prints bequeathed by another enthusiastic mountaineer, Robert Wylie Lloyd (1868-1958) to the British Museum's Department of Prints and Drawings is unrivalled outside and possibly inside Switzerland, containing as it does some of Turner and Towne's finest Swiss watercolours and about 2000 coloured prints of Switzerland by Swiss artists dating from before 1840. The British Museum's Department of Coins and Medals similarly possesses the outstanding collection of Swiss coins and medals assembled in the last century by the Reverend Chauncy Hare Townshend (d.1868) and the collection presented in the course of the 1860s by Count J.F.W. de Salis, a member of one of the oldest Anglo-Swiss families, which still maintains its links with Bondo and Soglio in the Val Bregaglia, Graubünden. Examples from most of these collections are to be found in this book.

The British Library continues, when it can, to acquire Swiss antiquarian material. Amongst the precious incunable printed books acquired in 1977 from the library formed at Broxbourne by Albert Ehrman was a beautifully preserved example of the first book to be printed in Geneva, in 1478, the *Livre des Sains Anges*. The Map Library regularly obtains by exchange modern official Swiss mapping - widely recognised as the best in continental Europe – down to a scale of 1:25000. Until very recently, every effort was made to purchase significant modern books published in all the languages of Switzerland as they appeared, and up to the past few years there has been close to blanket coverage. The increasing pressures on acquisitions' budgets and the astronomical rise in the price of antiquarian items have, however, led to a severe reduction and, in the case of antiquarian items, a complete halt in new acquisitions. If the British Library's proud tradition as one of the world's great repositories for Swiss material is to be maintained over the next few years, it will only be through generous support from outside institutions, companies and private individuals.

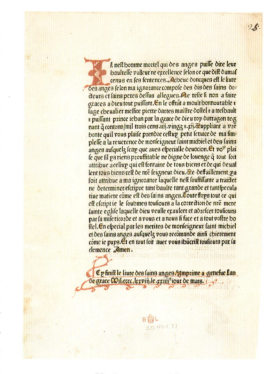

Closing page, with colophon, of the *Livre des Sains Anges* (Geneva: Adam Steinschaber, 1478). *1B 38406*

The King's Library in the British Museum, constructed 1823-7.

1 # *SWITZERLAND 700*

The Rütli Oath as depicted
by Jakob Stampfer in the
mid-sixteenth Century
(twice actual size)

[III.3.34]

1.1 *The Oath of Rütli and the Creation of Switzerland*

VUE DE LA PRAIRIE, DITE RUTLIN, SUR LE LAC DES QUATRE CANTONS,
Endroit où les trois Suisses formerent, en 1507, la généreuse résolution d'affranchir leur Patrie du joug qui l'opprimoit.

View of the meadow of Rütli on Lake Lucerne, *circa* 1780. From King George III's Topographical Collection. *K. Top. 85. 78*

Early in the August of 1291, representatives of the communities of three rural, thickly-forested valleys in a mountainous region at the south-western extremity of the German-speaking world met to renew an alliance stipulating mutual assistance in the maintenance of the judicial autonomy within the Holy Roman Empire that they believed, with varying degrees of reason, had been granted to them earlier in the century. Since about 1220 the valleys of Uri, Schwyz and Unterwalden had prospered from the expanded traffic across the Gotthard, the only North-South pass in the central Alps directly linking Germany with Italy. They had no desire to share their profits with, or to submit to the supervision of, the low-born and non-local representatives of their immediate feudal overlords, the Habsburgs. The date of the original alliance between Uri, Schwyz, Nidwalden and Obwalden (the last two collectively known as Unterwalden) is not known. The surviving treaty itself was only discovered in the archives of Schwyz in 1760. The form of their pact was not original, being found elsewhere in southern Germany and, in previous centuries, in the Italian mountains and plains south of the Gotthard and in no way was it tantamount to a declaration of independence. By 1470, however, legend had transformed the treaty into an oath taken, at some time between 1290 and 1315, on the meadow of Rütli (also called Grütli) overlooking Lake Lucerne, by Fürst for Uri, Stauffacher for Schwyz and Arnold for Unterwalden. It was only in the course of the nineteenth century that 1 August 1291 became generally accepted as marking the foundation of the Swiss Confederation, commonly known in German as the *Eidgenossenschaft* or, in literal translation, Society of the Oath.

Reproduction of the Pact of 1291 on a recent Swiss stamp.

[III.4.37]

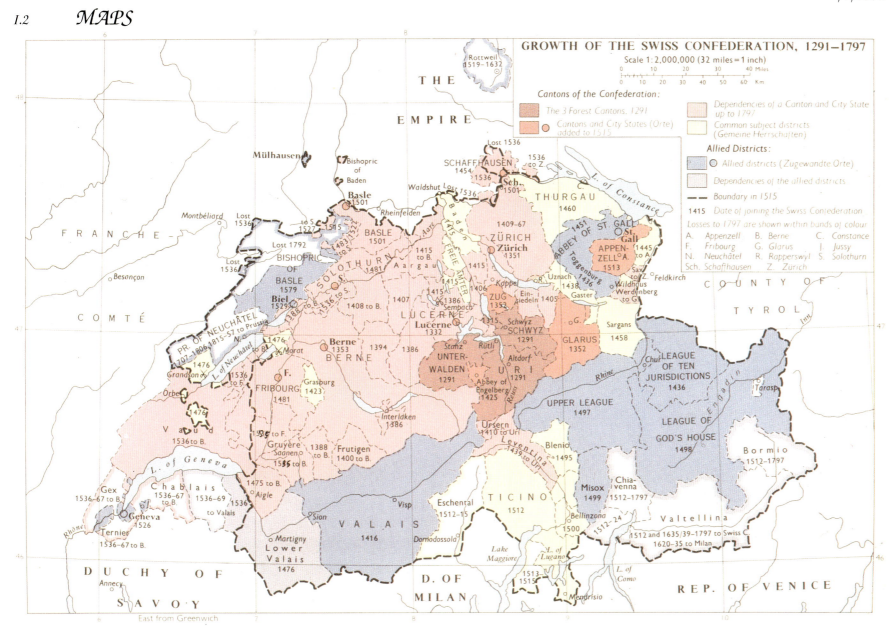

I.2.1   *Switzerland 1291 - 1797*

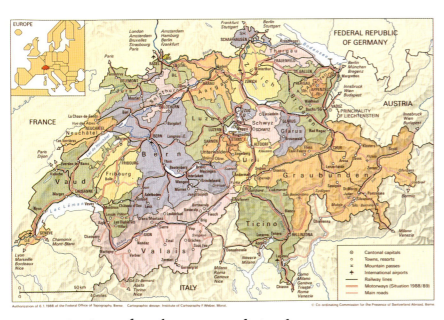

I.2.2   *Switzerland 1989: political*

I.2.3   *Switzerland 1989: linguistic and population*

1.3 *A Swiss Chronology – 1200-1991*

ca. 1220 Dramatic increase of commercial traffic over the Gotthard following the construction of the 'Devil's Bridge' over the Schöllenen Gorge in the district of Uri.

1231 Uri granted autonomy inside Holy Roman Empire.

1254-73 Absence of generally recognised Holy Roman Emperor sees growth of *de facto* local autonomy in the Alpine districts.

Aug 1291 First known league of Uri, Schwyz and Nidwalden renewing earlier alliance in support of their local autonomy.

Dec 1291 Obwalden joins the league.

1315 The Swiss defeat of Leopold Duke of Austria at Morgarten brings the allies to European attention.

1332-53 Accession of Lucerne (1332), Zurich (1351), Glarus (1352) and the powerful, aristocratic city state of Berne (1353).

1386 The Swiss confederates defeat the Habsburg Leopold II of Swabia at Sempach and strengthen their hold over the central plateau.

1403 Uri begins expansion southwards over the Gotthard.

1415 Confederate conquest of Aargau from Frederick of Austria.

1436-50 Civil war inside Confederation, principally between Zurich and Schwyz, reflects increasing tensions between urban and rural cantons.

1439 Cession of the Leventina Valley by Milanese to Uri.

1451 Abbot of St. Gallen allies with Confederation.

1460 Conquest of Thurgau from Austria gives access to Lake Constance.

1474-8 Stunning victories over Charles the Bold, Duke of Burgundy, at Grandson (2 March 1476), Morat/Murten (22 June 1476) and Nancy (5 January 1477) establish European reputation of Swiss arms.

1478 Victory over Milanese at Giornico.

1481 Admission of Solothurn and Fribourg to Confederation.

1497 Grey Leagues (Graubünden/Grisons) ally with Confederation.

1499 Peace of Basle, ending 'Swabian War', effectively frees Switzerland from Holy Roman Empire.

1501 Basle and Schaffhausen join Confederation.

1503 Bellinzona ceded to Swiss.

1511-15 Extensive Swiss and Allied conquests in north and north-east Lombardy from Milan.

1513 Appenzell joins Confederation which now contains 13 cantons. No further cantons admitted until 1803.

1513 Swiss victory over French at Novara.

1515 Swiss defeat by French at Marignano.

1516 "Perpetual" peace with France confirms most Swiss conquests, allows French to recruit troops in Switzerland, and implies Swiss international neutrality. Most notable renewals: 1521, 1663, 1725, 1777.

1519-24 Ulrich Zwingli introduces Reformation in Zurich. Several cantons and allies in eastern Switzerland also accept Reformation.

1524 Catholic 'Forest Cantons' of Lucerne, Uri, Schwyz, Unterwalden and Zug ally against Zurich and Reform movement.

1528 Reformation in Berne and

1529 Basle (under Oecolampadius).

J. L. Aberli, View of Berne from the North, *circa* 1750.
From King George III's Topographical Collection

K. Top. 85. 55.e.4.

1531	Religious civil war. Zwingli killed at Battle of Kappel (11 October).
1536	Berne seizes Vaud, Chablais and Lausanne (which adopt protestantism) from Savoy, and allies with Geneva.
1536	Guillaume Farel introduces Reformation into Geneva.
1541-64	Calvin organises Geneva as a theocratic state and refuge for persecuted protestants.
1549	Union of Zwinglian and Calvinist churches.
1577	Counter-Reformation spearheaded by (St.) Carlo Borromeo sharpens internal divisions.
1602	Failure of final Savoyard attempt to re-conquer Geneva.
1620-39	Struggle for control of Valtelline between France and Habsburgs of Spain and Austria.
1647	Defensionale of Wyl provides for Swiss armed neutrality in international disputes.
1648	Switzerland formally ceases to be part of Holy Roman Empire (Germany) and thereby legally becomes a sovereign, independent state.
1653	Peasant revolt in central Switzerland.
1656	Civil War. The First 'Villmergen' War ends in Catholic victory.
1674	Federal diet formally declares its permanent neutrality. No further meeting of diet until 1776.
1702-14	Catholic and protestant Swiss mercenaries find themselves in opposing armies during War of Spanish Succession.
1707-8	Kings of Prussia succeed as princes of Neuchatel.
1712	Second 'Villmergen War' ends in protestant victory.
1723-37	Widespread unrest in French-speaking areas subject to Berne and in Geneva.

1740-80	Economic improvement. Swiss Enlightenment. Beginnings of Alpine tourism.
1792	Genevan Revolution. Geneva allies with France.
1797	Valtelline and many French-speaking areas detached from Confederation by French who invade Basle.
1798	French invade remainder of Switzerland and create centralised but politically unstable Helvetic Republic of 23 cantons.
1803	Following mediation by Napoleon, the new Confederation of 19 sovereign cantons represents partial return to situation of before 1798, but with no allied or subject lands.
1815	Creation of Confederation of 22 sovereign cantons including Geneva, Valais and Neuchatel, most with conservative governments. Perpetual neutrality internationally recognised. Cession of largely French-speaking former diocese of Basle to Berne.
1823	Under external pressure, freedom of press restricted and refugee liberals persecuted and expelled (also 1834, 1838).
1828-33	Liberal revolutions in many cantons.
1845	Growing power of liberal, anti-clerical cantons wanting a revised, centralised constitution leads seven Catholic cantons to conclude a special defensive league (*Sonderbund*).
1847	Federal diet declares *Sonderbund* illegal. The forces of liberal, centralist cantons under Guillaume Dufour are victorious in a brief civil war.
1848	New, centralised constitution modelled on that of USA, with Berne as federal capital.
1848-91	Swiss politics dominated by conflict between liberals and Catholic conservatives.
1848-57	International crisis over status of Neuchatel.

1853	Austrians blockade Ticino because of its toleration of Italian revolutionaries. This and economic recession provoke massive emigration.
1860-1910	Industrialisation and growth of service sectors of economy (tourism and banking) at expense of agriculture. Large-scale emigration continues.
1863	Foundation of Red Cross by Henri Dunant.
1870-1	Neutrality during Franco-Prussian war.
1874	Revision of constitution results in further centralisation, but also in the introduction of popular legislative referenda, henceforth a hallmark of Swiss democracy.
	International Postal Congress selects Berne as its headquarters. Over the following 70 years Switzerland becomes the favoured European home for numerous international organisations.
1882	Completion of Gotthard Railway for first time provides all-weather link between German and Italian Switzerland.
1914-18 1939-45	Despite certain internal tensions between language groups and the need for some concessions to powerful neighbours, Switzerland maintains its armed neutrality centred around the concept of the Alps as a 'National Redoubt'.
1919	Liechtenstein enters into customs union with Switzerland.
1971	Female suffrage at national level. Total internal female suffrage achieved only in 1990 with its introduction throughout Appenzell.
1974	Non-Swiss constitute 16% of population.
1974-9	Creation of new canton of Jura out of most of the French-speaking areas of the canton of Berne.
1980	Opening of St. Gotthard road tunnel.
1986	Swiss vote against joining U.N.

II SWITZERLAND AND THE SWISS

Arms of the Swiss Cantons and their allies
surrounding the German Imperial arms.
Woodcut from Petermann Etterlin's
Kronika (1507)   *[II.3.1]*

II.1.   'Their Diversity of Religion and Cantons'

[Francis Bacon, Essays, 1597-1625]

Within 30 years of 1291, Uri, Schwyz and Unterwalden won a European-wide reputation as a result of their unexpected successes against their powerful neighbours, theoretical overlords and occasional suzerains, the Habsburgs, who had also coveted control of and income from the road from the Gotthard. The fourteenth and fifteenth centuries saw the league of three valleys gradually being transformed into a loose confederation. Minor rulers, abbeys, bishops, towns, cities and districts of the central highland plateau chose to ally with the three valleys, or were occupied by their increasingly powerful forces. From about 1450 the individual districts began to call themselves cantons. By 1540 the Confederation had ceased to be purely German-speaking. As a result of successful wars against the Habsburgs, the duke of Burgundy and the dukes of Milan and Savoy, French and Italian-speaking areas had come under the sway of the German-speaking Swiss. The Confederation consisted of thirteen sovereign cantons, with widely differing constitutions, several subject territories ruled by one or more cantons, and allies, such as the republic of Geneva, the Grey Leagues (Graubünden), the counts of Gruyère, the bishops of Chur, and the abbots of St. Gallen, with their own subject territories. Already riven by internal dissensions, they were united only by an awareness of the economic and political benefits of their association and by concern at the ambition of powerful neighbours, notably France, the Habsburgs and Savoy. The diet was primarily an inefficient mechanism for ruling the subject lands that the cantons held in common.

The spread of the Reformation from Zurich, Basle and the allied republic of Geneva after 1522 added a further element of division and also accentuated the rivalry between the larger, generally protestant cities, desiring a more centralised constitution, and the rural cantons and smaller, Catholic towns, which feared domination by the cities. Even some of the rural cantons were splintered by religion, as the enduring division of the small canton of Appenzell into two halves demonstrates. Between 1530 and 1847 these religious and constitutional rivalries sparked off repeated civil wars. The religious tensions only finally subsided in this century.

The allies and subject lands, which included most of the French, Italian and Romansch-speaking parts of the Confederation, were finally established as equal, sovereign cantons following the invasion of Switzerland by the French revolutionary armies in 1798, Napoleon's 'mediation' in 1803 and further territorial and constitutional changes at the Congress of Vienna in 1814-5. The country, nevertheless, only became a relatively centralised, federal state in 1848, after the final defeat of the rural, Catholic and conservative cantons in the previous year. The constitution, modelled on that of the USA, was revised in 1874.

Medal commemorating the alliance of the
Catholic Cantons with Valais, 1696.
(twice actual size)   *[III.3.57]*

Yet particularism continued to be strong. There was a conservative revolt in Neuchatel in 1856-7 and opposition from several of the poorer, Catholic cantons to greater centralisation in 1874. This century has witnessed a sustained campaign for independence from Berne in the French-speaking part of that canton, most of which, formerly part of the bishopric of Basle, had been joined to Berne only in 1815 as compensation for Berne's loss of its colonies elsewhere in Switzerland. The struggle culminated, as recently as 1979, in the creation of Jura as the twenty-third (twenty-sixth including half cantons) canton of the Confederation. Its final borders are still under negotiation.

Switzerland has long been an example to the world of co-operation, tolerance and mutual respect between its different cultural groups. Nevertheless there are increasing threats to that tolerance of diversity. The linguistic intolerance of many German Swiss and the retreat of standard German in face of local Schwyzerdeutsch dialects in public life in northern and eastern Switzerland present an often near-impenetrable barrier to the integration and careers of the French, Italian and Romansch-speaking Swiss who are drawn to the larger cities there. At another level, modern technology and communications, by effectively abolishing the buffer of the Alps, have led to the disappearance of most local French dialects and directly exposed minority languages to subordination to and even, in places, to submersion by the Schwyzerdeutsch-speaking majority, despite strenuous official action to sustain the minority languages and their cultures.

Stamp commemorating
the creation of the Canton
of Jura. The arms
incorporate the crosier of
the Bishopric of Basle
and stripes representing
the districts of the
Jura region. *[III.4.34]*

II.1.1 ***Roman Luxury***

This rather sculptural lamp was found in Switzerland. It testifies to the sophisticated lifestyle enjoyed in the region, notably by the military veterans from throughout the Empire who were settled there in increasing numbers from the first century B.C. What is now northern Switzerland was never thoroughly romanized, although magnificent finds have been made at Augst (Colonia Augusta Raurica) near Basle. In the south-west, south and east, however, the continuing influence of Rome can be seen in the French, Italian and Romansch languages spoken there.

Silver-plated bronze Roman lamp, in the form of a boat with a child Hercules struggling with serpents. 1st Century A.D.   *B>M. GR. 1915.4-13.1.*

II.1.1

Moses receiving the tablets
of the law from the hand
of God (above) and
delivering the law to
Aaron and the children of
Israel (below)   *II.1.2*

II.1.2 *Monastic Treasures 1*

Silver-gilt head of
St. Eustace   *II.1.3a*

This awe-inspiring copy of the Bible was created at the Benedictine Abbey of St. Martin at Tours in about 840. It is one of the two earliest preserved illustrated Carolingian Bible manuscripts. The text is a revised version of the Vulgate, made between 796 and 801 by Alcuin of York, appointed abbot of St. Martin's by the Emperor Charlemagne, who had brought him from England to supervise the education of his immediate family and of his kingdom. The Caroline minuscule script in which the body of the text is written is a fine example of the typical hand of the period. The Bible contains four magnificent full-page miniatures with designs that probably ultimately derive from a Late Antique model. Some twenty different scribes worked on the manuscript, which offers a measure of the importance of the industry of book production at Tours.

From at least the 16th until the 18th century the book belonged to the monastery of Moutier Grandval, then in the diocese of Basle. It is indeed possible that this was its original destination, as the Tours scriptorium routinely made manuscripts for use in other foundations. Moutier Grandval was one of a number of Swiss monasteries founded in the seventh century by Irish monks, of which the best-known is St. Gallen. Their cultural importance was matched by their political influence until the late eighteenth century. Moutier Grandval was dissolved in 1792 and the Bible passed into private hands until 1836 when it was sold to the British Museum.

'Moutier Grandval' Bible, c.840.   *Add. MS 10546*

II.1.3 *Monastic Treasures 2*

Wooden head of
St. Eustace   *II.1.3b*

The cult of relics, fostered by a desire to be near the bones or attributes of a saint, is as old as Christianity. This reliquary or relic container in the form of St. Eustace's head may have been commissioned for the Cathedral Treasury of Basle. The finished appearance of the wooden head suggests that the silver gilt head that for centuries covered it was an afterthought, though it must be close in date, and about 1200. Many such reliquaries in the form of a head, or *chefs*, covered with beaten silver and enriched with precious stones, are known to have been created, particularly in the German lands from the 12th century onwards. The German, or more properly upper Rhenish, workmanship of the St. Eustace head is characteristic of Basle, despite the city's vicinity to the Franco-German linguistic and cultural border and the fact that the diocese of Basle extended over French-speaking areas.

The wooden core for the head was hollowed out to contain several relics. When the reliquary was being conserved in 1956 these were found wrapped in fragments of silk and identified by vellum labels: among them were bones believed to have come from St. Eustace's skull. Like many other early medieval reliquaries, it therefore embodied the relic to the faithful while the relic itself was hidden from view. The relics have since been returned to Basle.

Silver-gilt head reliquary of St. Eustace, about 1200, formerly in the Cathedral Treasury in Basle, Switzerland wtith the wooden core for the head.

IB.M. M&La 50, 11-27.1.

II.1.4 *Trade and a German-speaking City*

By 1370 the Swiss allies, embracing Lucerne, Zurich and the powerful aristocratic city state of Berne as well as Uri, Schwyz and Unterwalden, were referring to themselves as an *Eidgenossenschaft* or confederation. The German language predominated. Zurich, which was important enough to be classed as an Imperial free (i.e. effectively independent) city, had signed a perpetual alliance with the 'Forest Cantons' of Uri, Schwyz, Unterwalden and Lucerne, in 1351.

In this charter, sealed on 13 March 1376 and written in German rather than Latin, the burgomaster, council and burgesses offer their protection to merchants who enjoyed special privileges because of their importance: Zurich derived its not inconsiderable wealth from manufacturing and from its silk trade with Italy by way of the Gotthard. By 1376 its government was dominated by the merchant guilds and was to remain so into the nineteenth century. Grants such as these were essential to the city's continuing prosperity which is reflected in the sophistication and fine workmanship of the excellently-preserved seal showing its three patron saints, Felix, Exuperantius and Regula rather gruesomely holding their heads in the hands.

II.1.4:
Detail showing shield.

Manuscript charter on vellum with black wax seal..

Add. Ch. 34939

II.1.4

II.1.5   *A French and German-speaking City*
         and an Independent Ally

Gold pattern of a sol of
Count Michael of Gruyére
1552.
(twice actual size)   [III.3.44]

The illustration shows Fribourg dominated then as now by the spire of its cathedral. Fribourg lies on the linguistic border between French and German. Its accession, with Solothurn, to the Confederation in 1481 nearly provoked a civil war, so fearful were the rural Forest Cantons of domination by the cities should more be admitted. The margin contains the arms of the counts of Gruyère who were allies of the Swiss and not full members of the Confederation until 1552-5 when the county was occupied by and partitioned between Fribourg and Berne following the extinction of the ruling dynasty.

II.1.5

II.1.5
Johannes Stumpf,
*Gemeiner loblicher
Eydgnoschaft, Stetten,
Landen und Völckern
chronicwirdiger thaaten
beschreibung . . . zum
anderen mal in der truck
gäben an vilen orten
gebesseret, gemeeret . . . biss
auff diss gegenwirtig 1586
jar durch J.R. Stumpff*
(Zurich, 1586)
ff. DXXVI-DXXVII.
9304.g.15

The *Schweytzer Chronik* by Johann Stumpf (1500-76) was the most popular and detailed early printed history and description of Switzerland, though significantly for the nature of Swiss self-awareness at the time, the first two sections deal with France and Germany. This 'description of the towns, lands, people and notable deeds of the common, praiseworthy confederation', to translate its full title, contains about 4000 woodcut maps, battle scenes, portraits, coats of arms and views of Swiss towns, all of the latter being based, for the first time in a printed book, on observation. First published in 1548 it went into several editions over the following decades.

II.1.6   *Switzerland in Italy*

After 1403 the Swiss cantons led by Uri, which wished to secure total control of the Gotthard and of the commercial routes to Milan from Germany, repeatedly sent forces into Italy. Their initial successes, which brought them almost to the shores of Lago Maggiore by 1411, were reversed by Milanese forces at Arbedo in 1422. Uri managed to retain the Leventina valley immediately south of the Gotthard, which was formally ceded by Milan in 1439, but it was only victory over the Milanese at Giornico (1478) that finally secured the Swiss position in that valley – and left them casting envious eyes on the strategically-placed fortress town of Bellinzona, which they had briefly occupied before 1422, and the districts and lakes beyond.

This map shows the area that they coveted. It is the earliest relatively large-scale printed map of a part of Europe (at a scale of nearly five miles to the inch) and was printed in Milan by a Bavarian in April 1490. Only one other example of this impression (and two of a second impression) are known. So novel was map printing that the wood cutter was unaware of the need for the design on the block to be reversed, with the result that the map itself is a

II.1.6   II.1.6 (reversed image)

mirror-image. Nor was he able to correct this at the second attempt. The map itself, however, reaches a level of accuracy not to be seen again on printed maps of the region for another 200 years. It shows Italy from the Leventina and Mesocco to Pavia with the rivers, the principal means of communication in the Alps, biting their way through the mountain valleys to the lakes.

Domenico Bellio (c.1450-1530), a humanist scholar from the village of Maccagno on the east shore of Lago Maggiore, and author of the accompanying tract on the Lake, claimed to have done the surveying himself in the course of a few days in 1489. He probably also had access, as tutor to the children of an important Milanese family, to accurate manuscript maps prepared for the Sforza dukes of Milan for military purposes. By 1515 the Swiss and their allies from Valais and the Grey Leagues (Graubünden) had occupied half of the lands shown on the map, most of which have remained Swiss ever since.

Domenico Bellio alias Macaneus [Map of Lago Maggiore and neighbouring lakes]. 27 x 20.4 cm. Scale ca. 1: 300000. First impression. In *Chrographya Verbani Lacus* (Milan: Ulrich Scinzenzeler, April 1490).

1A 26721

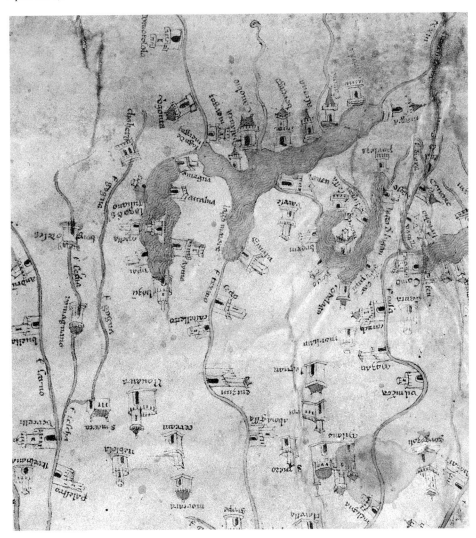

Detail showing the environs of Lago Maggiore from a manuscript map of Italy ('Italie provincie modernus situs') produced in northern Italy in about 1450.

Cotton Roll XII.44

II.1.7 *Swiss Pride*

As they expanded in territory, wealth and reputation, so the existing cantons became more reluctant to share their power and riches with others. In 1513, with the acceptance of Appenzell, the Confederation counted thirteen cantons (Uri, Schwyz, Unterwalden, Zug, Glarus, Berne, Lucerne, Zurich, Fribourg, Solothurn, Basle, Schaffhausen, Appenzell). No more were added for nearly 300 years. Even important cities such as Geneva did not progress beyond 'allied' status with restricted rights inside the Confederation.

The sauntering military standard-bearers and shields on this frontispiece to a tract of about 1525 encouraging the Swiss to assist pious evangelical Christians express the confidence of the time. The large, central crowned Imperial arms surrounded by the order of the Golden Fleece is a reminder that the Confederation legally remained a part of the Holy Roman Empire until 1648.

Ein zuversigtig ermanung an die redlichen erberen starcken vnd christlichen herren obern vnd vnderthon gemainer Eydgnoschafft (genant Schwytzer) das sy trewlich helffen handhaben Ewangelische vnd frumme christen (Basel (?), c.1525).   3908.f.34 (12)

II.1.7

II.1.8 *Reformation and Civil Strife*

From the 1520s, religion became another cause for conflict within the Swiss Confederation. In January 1523 Ulrich Zwingli (1484-1531) of Glarus, since 1518 the people's priest in the principal church of Zurich, the Grossmünster, won the full support of the town's city council for his 67 articles of faith, based on a literal interpretation of the gospels. These were immediately imposed inside Zurich and soon gained many adherents in other, generally urban cantons, notably Basle and Berne, while Zwingli himself in effect became Zurich's leader. The five rural cantons of Uri, Schwyz, Unterwalden, Zug and Lucerne, however, took alarm at his doctrines and at his efforts to centralise power in Switzerland around Berne and Zurich. Tension was high in 1530 as Zwingli, in a Swiss equivalent of the famous Lutheran Confession of Augsburg, re-stated his religious opinions for the benefit of Emperor Charles V, still legally the suzerain lord of the Confederation.

This German translation of Zwingli's statement of faith was printed by Zwingli's close friend, Christoffel Froschouer, the leading Zurich printer of the time. A youthful Charles V is portrayed on the cover. The defiant appeal – note the motto 'Die warheyt sol den sig haben' ('truth will prevail') – failed to sway Charles, who had already allied with the Catholic cantons. War broke out and within 18 months Zwingli had been slain in battle at Kappel south of Zurich. The religious divisions continued, however, and were further sharpened in the 1530s with the introduction of protestantism in Geneva and much of French-speaking Switzerland.

Ulrich Zwingli, Zu Karoln Roemischen Keyser jetzund uff dem Rychstag zu Ougsburg Bekentnuss des Gloubens durch Huldr. Zuinglium (Zurich: Christoffel Froschouer, 1530).   3906.a.41

II.1.8

II.1.9 Switzerland's Fourth Language

German, French, Italian and Romansch are spoken in Switzerland. Romansch or, more properly, Rhaeto-Romansch, is the only one not to be spoken beyond its frontiers. A Romance tongue, it is said to be descended from a fusion of Rhaetian and the colloquial Latin spoken by romanised Celts who fled to the mountains of Rhaetia in face of the Germanic invasions that followed the withdrawal of Roman forces from Switzerland. It is a peasant language spoken in widely-differing dialects in the eastern canton of Graubünden, where German and Italian are also spoken. Protestantism early gained a hold and catechisms, such as this, which were intended by their protestant authors to instil the gospels into children through questions and answers, are the earliest form of printed literature in Romansch.

Ioannes Planta da Samedan *Un cuort nuzaivel e bsognius Catechismus* (Poschiavo: Cornelius & Antonius Landuolphs, 1582). *4411.aaa.50 (2).*

Portrait of Ulrich Zwingli
by Jakob Stampfer, 1531
[III.3.35]

II.1.10 *Religious War and Peace*

In 1712 war broke out between the Abbot of St. Gallen and the cantons of Berne and Zurich. The immediate cause was a dispute between the Abbot and his subjects in the upper Thur Valley, or Toggenburg, who were seeking a greater degree of autonomy and religious toleration; but when the Catholic cantons of central Switzerland declared their support for the Abbot, the stage was set for a wider conflict in which Catholic and protestant cantons were ranged against each other.

The decisive battle of the campaign was fought at Villmergen, in the Aargau, on 25 July 1712. In this bloodiest battle of all the Swiss religious wars, the forces of Berne triumphed over the Catholics, who lost more than 2,000 dead. The peace signed at Aarau in the following month put an end to the hegemony of the Catholic cantons in favour of the more numerous protestants.

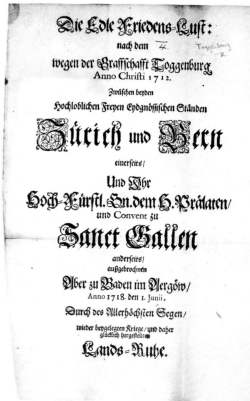

II.1.10

Medal commemorating Berne's victory in the
second Villmergen War by J. de Beyer, 1712.

[III.3.59]

The Abbot of St. Gallen, Leodegar Bürgisser, held aloof from these negotiations, and it was not until 1718 that his successor could be persuaded to make peace at Baden. This pamphlet celebrates the return of peace in a bombastic poem by Johann Rudolph Ziegler, later a canon of the Grossmünster in Zurich. The accompanying engraving by Johann Melchior Füssli, a relative of the Anglo-Swiss artist Henry Fuseli (see III.1.6), is unfortunately missing from this copy.

Johann Rudolph Ziegler, *Die edle Friedens-Lust: nach dem wegen der Graffschafft Toggenburg Anno Christi 1712 … aussgebrochnen aber zu Baden in Aergöw, anno 1718. den 1. Junii . . . wieder beygelegten Kriege und daher glücklich hergestellten Lands-Ruhe* (Zurich?,1719). 9305. aa.8 (4)

II.1.11 *The Old Regime in Switzerland*

This map gives some idea of the constitutional complexity of the Swiss Confederation before the changes wrought following the French Revolution. Different colours distinguish the protestant (blue) from the Catholic (pink) cantons, the territory of their allies (green) and the subject lands of the cantons and of their allies (yellow). The map would have become still more complicated had an attempt been made to distinguish between the rural cantons (e.g., Appenzell) with their popular assemblies, urban cantons dominated by guilds, like Zurich, and those dominated by aristocratic families like Berne; between allies that were republics (e.g. Geneva), abbeys (e.g. St. Gallen) or principalities (e.g. Neuchatel) and large (e.g. Graubünden) or small (e.g. Payerne); or between the subject bailliwicks ruled by the allies (e.g. Valtelline by the Graubünden) and those ruled by all the cantons except Appenzell (e.g. Locarno) or only some cantons (e.g. Grandson ruled by Berne and Fribourg). Each ally, moreover, had a different form of relationship with each of the cantons. Before 1798, Graubünden, literally translated as Grey Leagues and also known as Grisons, was a miniature Switzerland in itself, being a loose confederation of three near-sovereign leagues (God's House League, the League of Ten Jurisdictions and the Grey or Upper League) each containing numerous German, Romansch and Italian-speaking autonomous districts and subject territories. The leagues had become allied to the Swiss Confederation in the course of the fifteenth century.

The map derives from Guillaume Delisle's map of 1715, but despite its French title and appearance, it was published in England. John, Field Marshal Earl Ligonier (1680-1770) to whom the map is dedicated was a Huguenot who had been educated in Switzerland and rose to become Commander-in-Chief of the British army and Master General of the Ordnance, while Rouvier who published the map may have been Swiss. Before his death in 1762, the map was revised by John Rocque, arguably the best-known British cartographer of his time, who had been born in Geneva. The shields of the cantons and their allies, the references to William Tell and the column of soldiers below the cartouche add Swiss touches which would have been easily understood by contemporaries. The joined hands were a widely-accepted symbol for the Swiss Confederation before the formal adoption of the white cross on the red background in the nineteenth century. This particular copy of Rouvier's map belonged to George III.

Abraham Rouvier, 'Carte de Suisse où sont les treize cantons, leurs alliés et leurs sujets, dressée, rectifiée et augmentée sur les meilleurs auteurs'. 'T. Kitchin Sculp.' 'Published by A. Rouvier 1760 According to Act of Parliament.' 50 x 66 cm. ca. 1: 520000.   *K. Top. 85. 24.*

II.1.12 *A Federation or a Confederation of States?*

Federal Swiss forces
besieging Neuchatel
royalists, 1856
II.1.12 : p.145

After the French invasion of 1798, Switzerland underwent dramatic constitutional changes. From a unitary Helvetic Republic (1798-1803), modelled on France, it became a modified confederation of virtually independent states after 1803. Certain of the most important changes of the revolutionary period were retained after the fall of Napoleon in 1814-5. The status of the allies and of the former subject lands as fully-fledged cantons was confirmed, and areas such as Valais and Neuchatel that had been incorporated into France were returned to Switzerland, the total number of cantons rising from 13 to 22 (24 including half cantons). Partly in reaction to its tutelage by France after 1798, a strong feeling of distinctive Swiss identity also became widespread and Swiss citizenship finally took the place of purely cantonal citizenship. Old loyalties, however, also died hard particularly in the rural, conservative Catholic cantons. It took a brief civil war in 1847 to defeat their attempt through a special alliance, the *Sonderbund*, to halt the movement towards closer union. Even after 1848, the new federal constitution was not universally popular.

This anonymous book records, in a highly emotional republican and federalist manner, the dramatic events that occurred in Neuchatel, on the borders of France in western Switzerland, in 1856-7. The kings of Prussia had been

The Republic of Neuchatel secured,
by S. Mognetti, 1856.   *[III.3.146]*
(slightly enlarged)

sovereign princes of Neuchatel since 1707, with a brief break during the Napoleonic wars, and continued so after 1815 despite Neuchâtel's new status as a full member of the Swiss confederation. In 1848 a revolution led to the declaration of a republic, and later that year the new federal constitution declared that all cantons were to have republican forms of government. The international community and Frederick William IV of Prussia refused to accept this verdict and late in 1856 his supporters in Neuchatel provoked a European crisis by trying to regain power by force. The firm response by the local militias and by Berne, actively supported by the British government, led the Prussian King finally to renounce his claims. The crisis consolidated the constitution of 1848.

L'Enthousiasme de la Suisse pour la cause de Neuchatel (Fribourg, 1858).   *9304.d.7*

II.1.13 *A Living Language*

Since 1938 Romansch has been recognised in the federal constitution as Switzerland's fourth national language. Volume two of a four-volume contemporary history of Romansch literature is included here to demonstrate that although the first language of barely 40,000 people, it is still alive and is being nurtured through the Romansch League. Official moves are also afoot actively to protect it through provisions in the revised constitution that is currently under negotiation and by encouraging the creation of a standard language, *Romantsch Grischun*, from an agreed amalgamation and codification of the variant dialects.

Gion Deplazes, *Funtaunas. Istorgia da la litteratura rumantscha per scola e pievi* (Cuira [Chur]: Lia rumantscha, 1987 –).   *ZA. 9. a. 3190*

II.2 *Arms and Neutrality*

A soldier from Rottweil.
G. della Torre,
Descriptio Helvetiae (1607)
[II.2.2]

Medal commemorating
the renewal of the
Franco-Swiss alliance
in 1663,
by J. Mauger, (1702).
(enlarged by 30%)
[III.3.169]

A series of stunning victories by Swiss infantrymen over the better-armed forces of the Habsburgs, the French and the Dukes of Burgundy and Milan from Morgarten in 1315 to Novara in 1513, by way of Grandson (1475), Morat (1476) and Giornico (1478) bestowed an awesome European reputation on Swiss arms. As a result the cantons found themselves being courted by most of the major European powers. Under the terms of their 'Perpetual' – and repeatedly renewed - Alliance with France (1516), the cantons agreed to allow the French king to recruit high-quality infantry regiments in return for commercial and political advantages (see medals III.3.36; 3.169, 170). In time they extended similar rights to other countries and Swiss soldiers served as mercenaries throughout Europe and the world. Repeated condemnations of mercenary service by Zwingli and others, general unease at the prospect of Swiss fighting Swiss; shame at being branded as mercenaries and official efforts to discourage recruitment by foreign powers inside the Confederation, were ineffectual in stopping the trade: treaty obligations could not be ignored and military service abroad provided the sole means, before the coming of mass tourism, for innumerable Swiss peasants to support their families and advance themselves despite the abject poverty of their homeland. Even today the Swiss Guard, recruited among the Catholic Swiss, continues to defend the Pope, though since 1859 the Swiss government has progressively forbidden all other forms of foreign service.

The virtual ending of foreign service was accompanied by a strengthening of Swiss neutrality, which already had a tradition of several centuries behind it. As early as 1470 some influential voices had been warning against further foreign entanglements, and the Perpetual Alliance stipulated a form of pro-French neutrality in international affairs. In 1647 with the Defensionale of Wyl the cantons jointly determined to garrison their frontiers against any external challenge to them or to their perpetual neutrality. Though not immediately recognised by others, totally disregarded by the French between 1798 and 1814 and subjected to strains and some abuses during the two world wars, armed neutrality has remained the cornerstone of Swiss foreign policy to this day.

Neutrality has been dictated by national self-interest and not, despite what some may choose to believe, by idealism or pacifism. It has been a response to the realisation that any active involvement in foreign disputes risked splintering a country with such pronounced internal religious and cultural-linguistic divisions and it has been accompanied by regular manoeuvres, shooting festivals and mobilisations in wartime to protect its frontiers (see III.3.173, III.4.35). Even today three weeks military service about every two years is compulsory for almost all Swiss males under 50, each of whom has the right to possess a rifle.

The principle of neutrality has led Switzerland to remain outside the European Community (though not the European Free Trade Association – see III.4.33) and even the United Nations. The latter's European home is, however, in Geneva which houses many other international agencies, such as the International Postal Union, which have been attracted to the country because of its traditional neutrality. Switzerland has been very actively involved in these less political organisations, and particularly in the humanitarian ones such as the Red Cross, founded in 1863 by Henri Dunant of Geneva, which has a Swiss flag in reversed colours as its symbol (see III.4.21, III.4.39-44).

III.4.44

Nevertheless the relevance of neutrality and even of the army in the post-Cold War era and in a Europe that is becoming ever more economically and politically integrated is now being questioned inside Switzerland. In a recent referendum, one third of the participants voted for the abolition of the Swiss army: a situation that barely a decade ago would have been almost unthinkable.

Medal commemorating
Swiss neutrality during
the Franco-Prussian War,
by C. Richard, 1871.

[III.3.173]

II.2.1 *Point d'Argent, Point de Suisses*

The disastrous defeat of the Swiss by the French at Marignano near Milan in September 1515, which put a stop to Swiss expansionist dreams, was at first seen as no more than a passing incident. In no way did it diminish the prestige of Swiss troops – if they could be got to fight. Matthäus Schiner (c.1465-1522), Cardinal-Bishop of Sion (see also coins III.3.23, 24), the Cardinal Wolsey of Swiss history, yearned for his countrymen to capture Milan as a means of protecting the papacy from French domination and of paving the way for his eventual election as Pope. Henry VIII of England, Emperor Maximilian and the young King Charles of Spain (later Emperor Charles V) saw the capture of Milan as part of a grand strategy for attacking France from all sides.

In this declaration of 7 November 1516, Schiner and Jean Baptiste Tisson, Comte de Decian, as Imperial envoys, confirm the readiness of Henry, Maximilian and Charles, in compliance with their treaty of 29 October, to pay the Swiss an annual sum of 30,000 gold florins in return for their 'friendship and benevolence' – a euphemistic reference to their agreement to invade the Milanese once again. If this is insufficient, they will pay a further 6000 gold florins, and if even this is not enough, they will consider the matter further. The declaration, written in a handsome humanist hand, is signed and sealed by both envoys, with Schiner's signature ('Matheus Card*inali*s Sidenien*sis*) and armorial seal (also to be seen on his coins) on the left.

The desperation to secure the help of the Swiss at almost any price stemmed from the knowledge that the cantons, several of whom were reluctant to get involved in Italy, were simultaneously negotiating with the King of France. Three weeks after the sealing of this declaration, on 29 November 1516, the Swiss concluded a treaty of perpetual peace with France. In return for one million crowns (about 200,000 florins) and the confirmation of continued possession of virtually all the Milanese lands they had conquered before 1513, the Swiss undertook to refrain from hostile activities against France and to allow the French to recruit in Switzerland. This treaty, continually renewed, became a cornerstone of Swiss and particularly Catholic Swiss foreign policy until the French Revolution.

Declaration by the envoys of Maximilian I and Charles I of Spain relating to payments due to the Swiss under the Treaty of London (29 October 1516), London, 7 November 1516.

Add. Ch. 1520

Testoon of Sion
with portrait of
Cardinal Schiner
(slightly enlarged)

[III.3.23]

II.2.1

II.2.2. *The Swiss Guard Portrayed*

Giovanni, Count della Torre and Bishop of Veglia served as papal ambassador, or nuncio, in Switzerland after 1595. A large part of his duties consisted of facilitating the recruitment of Swiss regiments in the Catholic cantons. In line with an old diplomatic tradition, he also compiled a description or 'relation' of Switzerland, distinct from his regular dispatches, to provide his masters with background information on the land where he had been serving. This copy was dedicated in May 1607 to Cardinal Scipio Borghese, the influential nephew of Pope Paul V.

The Cardinal was famous as a patron of the arts. The text is, accordingly, far more lavishly illustrated than was usual with such works. Apart from brief histories of the component parts of the Confederation, lists of towns and parishes and a rare, early engraved map of Switzerland, published in Rome in 1555 by Antonio Salamanca from Gilg Tschudi's survey of 1538, there are numerous watercolour depictions of towns, patrons saints, and Swiss heraldry. Most distinctively of all, soldiers in local dress are shown carrying banners with the arms of each of the Swiss districts. The town views, though colourful, are fairly routine copies of woodcuts in Stumpf's *Schweyzer Chronik* of 60 years earlier. The other illustrations, however, are of far higher artistic quality and have been attributed to the circle of Daniel Lindtmayer (1552-1606/7) of Schaffhausen. Lindtmayer, who probably died in Lucerne where della Torre was based, regularly supplied designs for stained glass windows, a Swiss speciality, to Franz Fallenter, the leading Swiss glass painter, and a stained window by Fallenter commissioned by della Torre in 1611, is now owned by the Swiss National Museum in Zurich.

The manuscript was acquired at auction in London by the British Museum in 1850.

Giovanni, Count della Torre, Bishop of Veglia, *Descriptio Helvetiae*, 1607.　　　*Add. MS 18285*

II.2.2: The Standard Bearer of Zug.

II.2.3 ## *While in Foreign Service*

Johannes Willading (1630-1698), a scion of a leading Bernese family, created this decorative plan of a famous Christian victory over the Turks while in the service of the Holy Roman Emperor. The plan, which was originally accompanied by another plan that is now lost, simultaneously shows several stages of the battle, fought on the banks of the River Raab in Hungary on

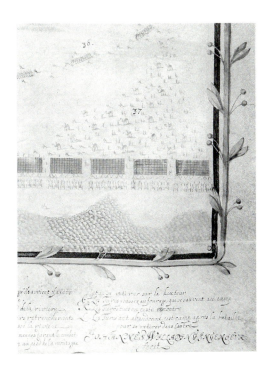

II.2.3

1 August 1664, with the different episodes numbered and explained below. The cartouche on the right shows a Turkish captive kneeling before a Christian commander, with a camel lending an exotic touch. The plan, which recalls French commemorative maps of the time, was probably prepared for a French general and is lavish in its praise of the role played by the regiments sent by Louis XIV to the assistance of the Emperor. Like many able Swiss, Willading had at first to go abroad to find employment as a military engineer. Unusually, however, after years of service in central Europe and the Venetian empire, he was employed from 1668 as Berne's sole, full-time military engineer.

'De plus la situation du lieu est icy representé où les armées Chrestiennes . . . ont en fin . . . mis en confusion [les Turcs]' [i.e. plan of the Battle of Szent Gotthard, 1 August 1664]. 'Johannes Willading Ingenieur fecit'. 54 x 128 cm. Scale: 100 pas communs (= 13 cm.) [i.e. ca. 1:2000].

Eg. MS 1523

II.2.4 *Neutrality Versus Foreign Service*

In June 1689, William III needed Swiss troops for the war in Ireland against James II and Louis XIV of France. He sent Thomas Coxe to the protestant cantons to negotiate their hire. The Swiss, though sympathetic, were fearful of the reaction of their powerful neighbour, Louis XIV, and determined not to infringe their neutrality and existing treaties, particularly with France. They drove a hard bargain. The conditions of service were regulated to the smallest detail in this draft by Coxe, incorporating Swiss and English amendments, and dating from shortly before the treaty was finally signed at Aarau on 23 August 1690.

Service anywhere but in Great Britain and Ireland, the Swiss insisted, would infringe their neutrality and treaties. They were prepared to supply two regiments, amounting to four thousand men, for a minimum of four years but only if the cantons received a considerable annual subsidy and the soldiers were from the start paid at the same rates as the King's Regiment of Guards (amended later to the French King's Guards who were better paid), with a bonus of 10% for every company that was above, or not far below, strength. Victory in the field merited a further bonus and a right to all their booty except artillery. They were to serve together, as far as possible, with their own chaplains, command structure and judges, with William selecting only their colonels. The cantons were to be safeguarded financially and militarily against a French revenge attack. Amidst the military provisions, were some broader commercial clauses, others to safeguard the inheritance of Swiss property in England and an enlightened obligation on William to finance 24 Swiss students through their studies at Oxford and Cambridge.

On 6 November William ratified the treaty – but only on condition that the Swiss agreed to serve his allies once he had no further need for them. This the cantons refused to agree to, fearing it would infringe their neutrality and treaties, enrage Louis XIV, lead Swiss to fight Swiss and earn them the 'titre honteux de mercenaires qui servent pour de l'argent au premier offrant'. The treaty remained inoperative, though in the next century protestant Swiss soldiers did serve with the British, particularly in French Canada.

Draft of convention for hire of Swiss troops between William III and Swiss Protestant cantons, July-August 1690. *Add. MS 38013, ff. 64-7.*

II.2.5 *Swiss Partisans in British Pay*

Following the French invasion of Switzerland in 1798, three Swiss regiments, of Bachmann, Roverea and Salis, accepted payment amounting to £141,560 from Britain in order to continue their struggle against the invader. Loosely described at the time as the 'Swiss' or 'Helvetic' Legion and clad in a distinctive green, over the next two years they fought side-by-side with British and other Allied troops in the Graubünden, Austria and Germany, and gained a considerable reputation for valour. In 1801 they were re-organised as de Watteville's regiment, which was only disbanded in 1816, having fought in Malta, Sicily, Spain and finally Canada.

This seal was almost certainly that of the Legion and well summarises its nature. At the centre are George III's arms as they were before 1801, when the French fleurs-de-lys were dropped, and surrounding them are the shields of the thirteen cantons of the old confederation: for these Swiss would have no truck with the puppet Helvetic Republic and its new cantons. The inscription 'Schweyzerisch Truppen Commando' ('Command of the Swiss Troops') reflects their good organisation, which was commented on at the time, and the fact that most of its men - largely aristocratic Bernese - could speak no English. The incorrect rendering of the St. Edward's crown suggests that the seal was cut locally.

II.2.5

Modern impression of the seal of the British Swiss Legion ('Schweyzerisch Truppen Commando'), c.1799.

Det. Seal CLXII.1.

II.3 *'Bright Liberty Triumphant'*

[Anna Seward, *Alpine Scenery*, 1785]

Switzerland has long been regarded as a bastion of liberty. The legend of William Tell and of a small mountain people's struggle against foreign oppression did much to establish this reputation. Over the centuries the nature of that liberty has evolved. For most of the sixteenth and seventeenth centuries Zurich and particularly Geneva became bastions of protestant liberty and refuges for protestants from throughout Europe. In the eighteenth and nineteenth centuries the cantons and the republics associated with Switzerland became bulwarks of constitutional liberty, providing conveniently-located free presses for the publication of a wide variety of seditious works that were banned in their countries of origin. The protection afforded to foreign exiles and Swiss printing presses frequently exposed the Swiss cantons and republics to the wrath of its powerful neighbours, which was, at times, courageously withstood at considerable cost to themselves. In this century, Switzerland has been seen as a stronghold of western democratic, as opposed to communist or fascist, liberty and values because of its long tradition of popular participation in government through referenda and popular assemblies, while innumerable foreign writers, musicians and artists have found in Switzerland the conditions of spiritual liberty necessary for the completion of their best works.

In this century the enormous increase in international migrant and refugee numbers has been perceived as a threat to the fabric of Swiss society. Since 1939, this has occasionally led to distinctly illiberal actions by Swiss authorities who were sometimes perhaps a little too fearful of retaliation from dictatorial neighbours, over-sensitive to the clamour of xenophobic groups inside Switzerland, and insufficiently sensitive to the fears of persecuted foreign minorities. Nevertheless, the largely justified association of Switzerland with liberty remains one of the country's major contributions to international society.

View of the monument to the three founders of Swiss Liberty erected on Altstadt Island, Lake Lucerne, in 1780 by the radical French writer Abbé Raynal (1713-96) who was himself a political refugee in the Confederation. From King George III's Topographical Collection.

K. Top. 85.79-b.

à Bâle chez Chr. de Mechel

VUE DE LA PETITE ISLE D'ALTSTADT SUR LE LAC DE LUCERNE, avec le MONUMENT que le célebre ABBÉ RAYNAL y a fait eriger à la gloire des trois premiers Fondateurs de la Liberté Helvétique.

II.3.1 *William Tell*

According to legend, the Habsburgs' administrator in Uri, Gessler, compelled William Tell, an upright peasant, to shoot an apple from his own son's head after Tell had refused to salute the hat on a stick which had been set up in Altdorf as a sign of authority. This he succeeded in doing, but he kept one arrow aside (to be seen sticking out of the bag on Tell's back) which he later used to kill Gessler. This precipitated the uprising that drove the Habsburg oppressors from the three cantons.

The legend probably dates back no earlier than the 1420s. It was first recorded, in a text based on an earlier source, in the *White Book* of Sarnen in 1470 at about the time that the Robin Hood legend first appeared in England. The story of the apple was stolen from Scandinavian mythology and the interpretation of events, compiled after more than a century of Swiss conflict with the Habsburgs, bears only a scant resemblance to the historical reality. Nevertheless William Tell was taken to be a historical character until late in the eighteenth century and his myth established the international association of Switzerland with liberty that has endured to this day.

The *Kronika* of Petermann Etterlin of Lucerne (1430/40-1509) is the earliest printed Swiss chronicle. It has some independent value for the events of the later fifteenth century and particularly the wars with Charles the Bold of Burgundy in which Etterlin was directly involved as a soldier and diplomat. For the earlier period, however, it is borrowed uncritically from earlier texts, most notably the *White Book* of Sarnen. The illustration showing Tell shooting the apple off his son's head, by an anonymous artist, is perhaps the most skilfully executed in the book and almost the only one to be used once only and to relate specifically to the text. The British Library possesses examples of both of the original states of Etterlin's chronicle.

Despite its weaknesses, the *Kronika* exerted an enormous influence on successive Swiss chronicles before Stumpf's (1548). The printer, Heinrich Petri of Basle, re- utilised this very woodblock to illustrate the account of William Tell in Sebastian Münster's *Cosmographia* of 1544. Republished in no less than 33 editions in different languages before 1600, the *Cosmographia* played a large part in popularising the legend of William Tell throughout Europe.

II.3.1

Petermann Etterlin, *Kronika von der loblichen Eydtgnoschaft ir harkommen und sust seltzam strittenn und geschichten* (Basel: Michael Furtter, 1507), f. xv   591.g. 1

II.3.2 A Refuge For Protestants

Geneva, under Calvin, became the 'Rome of Protestantism' and, as such, the leading city of refuge for those fleeing Catholic persecution. The Scottish reformer, John Knox (c.1515-1572), came to Geneva in the mid-1550s after the accession of the Catholic Mary Tudor to the English throne, serving as minister of the congregation of English exiles and contributing to the Geneva Bible (see II.6.2). So impressed was he with the Calvinist city-state, which he called 'the maist perfyt schoole of Chryst that ever was in the erth since the dayis of the Apostillis', that after 1559 he went on to become the dominant figure in the establishment of a particularly austere form of protestantism modelled on it in Scotland.

The portrait of Knox shown here, possibly based on a painting by Adrian Vanson, was specially commissioned by Beza for his *Icones* or *Verae Imagines* (*Images* or *True Portraits*), a series of illustrated lives of reformers, dedicated to James VI of Scotland (later James I of England). Indeed this portrait of Knox has become the generally accepted likeness of the reformer. Theodore de Beza (or Théodore de Bèze in French) (1519-1605), a close collaborator of Calvin's and his eventual successor, emphasised in his dedicatory preface the contribution made by Geneva to the churches of Scotland and England.

Theodore de Bèze, *Icones id est verae imagines virorum . . . illustrium etc. Apud I. Laonium* [Geneva] 1580. *611. e. 3*

IOANNES CNOXVS.

93

IOANNES CNOXVS, SCOTVS' GIFFORDIENSIS.

ETSI distincta fuerunt semper Angliæ & Scotiæ regna suis tũ finibus tum regibus, dixisse tantùm liceat fuisse nostra patrúmque memoria tum aduersus Christum initio consociata, tum ad Christum rursum mutuis operis adiuncta. Sicut autem illius aduersus veritatem conspirationis auctor quidem præcipuus fuit Romanus ille pontifex, administri verò Cardinales & pseud-Episcopi, totus ille denique pseudoclerus, ab illo haud secus quàm à suo numine dependens: sic ad ius illud suum recuperandum CHRISTVS fidos homines admirabili virtute instructos vtrobique excitauit. Ac de Anglis quidẽ dictum esto, à quibus ad Scotos transeũtibus primus occurrit magnus ille IOANNES CNOXVS, quem si Scotorum, in verò Dei cultu instaurando, velut Apostolum quendam dixero, dixisse me quod res est existimabo, & sequẽs vera ipsius vitæ narratio testabitur. Cnoxus igitur (vt manifestè appareat totum hoc admirabile Domini opus esse) ad Ioannis illius Maioris, celeberrimi inter Sophistas nominis, veluti pedes in Sanctandrȩæ oppido educatus, atque adeò sacerdos factus, apertáque celebri schola, quum iã videretur illo suo præceptore nihilo inferior Sophista futurus, lucem tamẽ in tenebris & sibi & aliis accẽdit. Siquidem Hieronymi & Augustini libros ibi nactus, ex eorũ scriptis, non fastidire modò, sed etiam redarguere multa vsque adeò liberè cœpit, Edimburgum prȩsertim regiam ciuitatem euocatus, vt Hamestonum vnicum tũc piorum asylum perfugere cogeretur. Ibi verò tandem

Ee. iij.

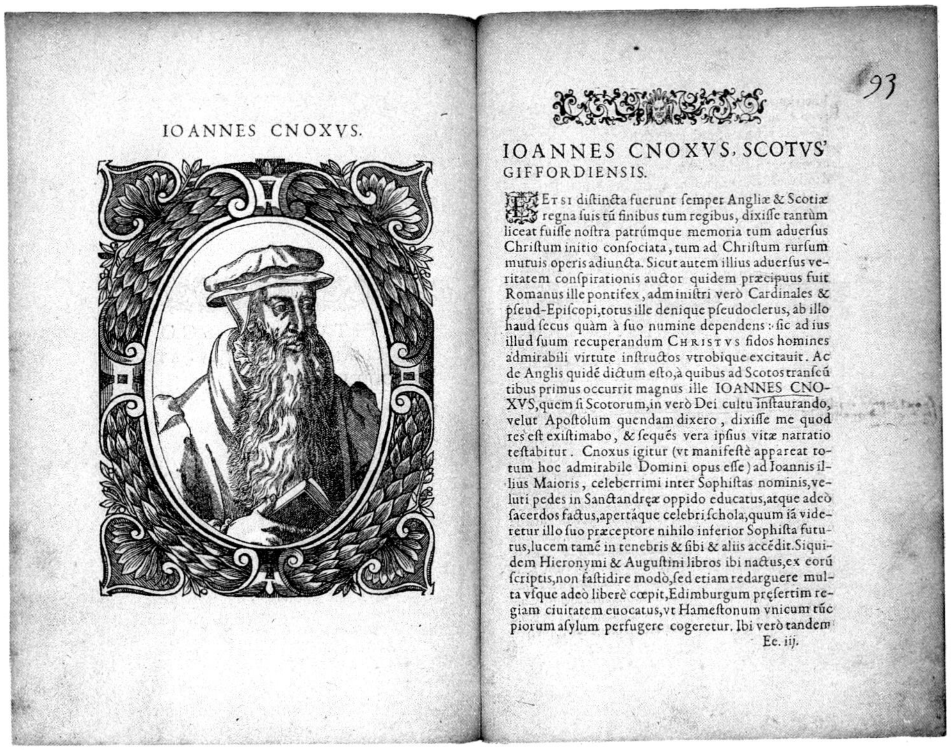

II.3.3 *"The Free Corner of Geneva"*

François Arouet de Voltaire (1694-1778) was offered asylum in Geneva after quarrelling with Frederick the Great of Prussia in Berlin and finding himself 'persona non grata' in his native country, France. The republican city-state seemed to offer a climate of freedom and toleration in pointed contrast to French absolutism, as Voltaire proclaimed to all and sundry, together with publishers for his works in the brothers Cramer. Voltaire settled in a property just outside Geneva as well as buying a house at Lausanne for the winter. He renamed his Geneva house 'Les Délices', an allusion to the delights of freedom and independence from courts and patrons. 'Les Délices', now the Voltaire Institute and Museum, soon became a Mecca for visitors who came to worship, or to gawp, at the shrine of Europe's most famous intellectual.

DE L'ESPRIT
DES
LOIX
OU DU RAPPORT QUE LES LOIX DOIVENT AVOIR AVEC LA
CONSTITUTION DE CHAQUE GOUVERNEMENT, LES MOEURS
LE CLIMAT, LA RELIGION, LE COMMERCE, &c.
à quoi l'Auteur a ajouté.
Des recherches nouvelles sur les Loix Romaines touchant les
Successions, sur les Loix Françoises, & sur les Loix féodales.

TOME PREMIER.

A GENEVE,
Chez BARILLOT, & FILS.

Title page of the
first edition of
Montesquieu's
De l'Esprit des Lois
(Geneva, 1748)
1233 f. 1.

One frequent visitor to 'Les Délices' during his stay in Geneva in 1756 was George Keate (1729-1797) and the two men remained in correspondence after the young Englishman's return to England. This letter to Keate is written in Voltaire's own hand and in his excellent English, acquired during a period of exile in England in 1726-8 which made a deep impression on him. He praises the political liberalism common to Geneva and England: 'Had I not fix'd the seat of my retreat in the free corner of Geneva, I would certainly live in the free kingdom of England'.

By the time he wrote this letter in 1760, however, Voltaire, having had several clashes with the Genevan ministers, who turned out not to be as advanced on the road to Enlightenment as he had supposed, had bought a property at Ferney, just across the French border, to which he removed for good in 1764.

In the course of the eighteenth century, several other French writers utilised the presses of Geneva to publish works that were too critical of the existing establishment to be published in France. Perhaps the most notable was Montesquieu's *De l'Esprit des Lois* which was first published in Geneva by Barillot et Fils in 1748.

Francois Arouet de Voltaire to George Keate, FRS, 16 January 1760. *Add. MS 30991, f.13*

II.3.4 *A Blast Against Tyrants*

Had Antonio Panizzi (1797-1879) not been a patriotic Italian and had he never plotted to overthrow the Habsburg Duke Francis IV of Modena, he would probably have remained a good, but unknown lawyer in his native Brescello in Northern Italy. Panizzi, like many patriotic young Italians, however, joined a secret society affiliated to the 'Carbonari' and did all in his power to overthrow his autocratic, Austrian-supported prince. He was discovered but managed to escape arrest and was able to flee.

En route for England, his future homeland, Panizzi remained in the Ticino sufficiently long to write and publish a blistering attack on Francis IV and his tyrannical regime. It was published in Lugano under the false imprint of 'Roberto Torres, Madrid'.

Portrait of
Antonio Panizzi
as a young man
by Antonio Berchet.
C.133.e.1

A tradition of printing anti-Austrian propaganda became established in Ticino in general and in particular at Capolago, on Lake Lugano, after 1815. At first it was connived at by the conservative Ticinese authorities except when Austrian pressure grew too great and forced them to expel the Carbonari and restrict press freedom. Following a liberal revolution in 1830 it was openly tolerated, even though, in 1853, it and further evidence of official Ticinese involvement in anti-Austrian activities in Italy led to ferocious Austrian counter-measures. All the Ticinese were expelled from Lombardy and a blockade was imposed on the canton. With starvation beckoning, the Ticinese were forced to find new countries to emigrate to – among them Australia and England – but the authorities and certain individuals remained firm: several Ticinese fought at Garibaldi's side in his campaign of 1859-60.

Antonio Panizzi arrived in England in May 1823. He was eventually engaged as a cataloguer by the British Museum Library and rose to become its Director and Principal Librarian. His lasting monument is the famous circular reading room.

Panizzi, who was knighted in 1869, came to regret having published his attack. He endeavoured to purchase and destroy as many copies as he could. Only two are known to survive. The one exhibited here is unique since it contains manuscript additions by Panizzi.

Sir Anthony Panizzi, *Dei processi e delle Sentenze contro gli imputati di lesa-maestà e di aderenza alle Sette prescritte negli Stati di Modena* (Madrid [Lugano] per Roberto Torres, 1823).   *C. 44. d. 1.*

II.3.5 ## Composed in Exile

At the outbreak of war in 1914 Stravinsky and his family were on one of their regular visits to Switzerland. They remained, first at Clarens, then at Morges, taking refuge from the war and from the turmoil in Russia culminating in the October Revolution of 1917, which brought to an end Stravinsky's direct links with his own country. *Les Noces* and *Renard* are among the major works dating from this period. Stravinsky's Swiss friends included the conductor Ernst Ansermet, who introduced him to the writer C.F. Ramuz; Ramuz provided the French translation of the text for *Les Noces*, and a collaboration between the two men in 1918 produced *L'histoire du soldat*.

II.3.5

In 1920 Stravinsky moved to France and *Pulcinella* is his last Swiss work. The idea for the ballet came from Diaghilev, who was anxious to draw Stravinsky back to the Ballets Russes. He provided copies of works by (or attributed to) Pergolesi, assembled from Italian libraries, and from the British Museum, with the suggestion that they should be arranged to provide a ballet with a *commedia dell'arte theme*. They drew from an initially reluctant composer pungent versions of this 'delightful eighteenth-century music', employing chamber music-like combinations of instruments from a small orchestra, with a concertino group of solo strings, and soprano, tenor and bass soloists singing from the pit. The work was first staged in Paris in May 1920 with choreography by Massine and designs by Picasso. Stravinsky has described it as 'my discovery of the past, the epiphany through which the whole of my late work becomes possible'.

Various sections of this sketch-book are dated, from September 1919 to a draft of the Finale signed 'Morges 11 April 1920'. It is written more or less in full score throughout, using pencil and various coloured inks and with the staves ruled in as and where needed, apparently with some speed, using the special roulette instrument designed by Stravinsky himself and described by Ramuz in his memoire of the composer.

Igor Stravinsky, Sketchbook for *'Pulcinella'*, 1919-1920.   *Zweig MS 94*

II.3.6 *Spiritual Freedom in a Disordered World*

Hermann Hesse (1877-1962), a German author and lyrical poet, best known in England for his novel *Steppenwolf* (1927), first lived in Switzerland as a child and returned there shortly before the outbreak of the First World War, which he fervently opposed. After 1919 he moved to Montagnola, southern Ticino, where he found the spiritual peace and liberty, in what seemed a schizophrenic and disintegrating Europe, to write. He adopted Swiss nationality in 1925. While being treated by Carl Jung (see II.5.11), he began painting and illustrating his poems with watercolours. These watercolours, of views towards Lake Lugano from his home, are typical. They illustrate a set of typewritten poems, collectively called *'Sommer 1933'* ['Summer 1933'], which he presented to the Austrian-Jewish author Stefan Zweig.

The British Library possesses manuscripts written in Switzerland by several other non-Swiss twentieth century writers. Hesse, however, is particularly representative of a large group of predominantly German-speaking writers and artists, in some ways resembling the Bloomsbury Group in England, who from the turn of the century attempted to 'return to nature' in the idyllic surroundings of Ticino, most famously on the hill overlooking Ascona which they renamed 'Monte Verità' ['Hill of Truth']. Since 1945 this fame, and that of Hermann Hesse personally, has contributed considerably towards the flood of German-speaking settlement that now characterises parts of the canton. Ticino has remained a favoured home for such German-speaking writers as Friedrich Dürrenmatt, Hans Habe, Golo Mann and Erich Maria Remarque.

Hermann Hesse, *'Sommer 1933'*.   *Zweig MS 157, ff.4,6ᵛ-7, 10, 12, 14*

II.4   *Alps and Tourism*

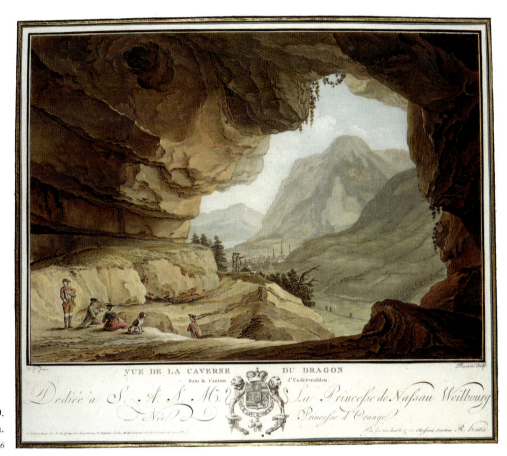

Tourists in the Alps, *circa* 1780.
From King George III's Topographical Collection.
8 Tab. c. 6

A promenade along the
Höheweg in Interlaken,
circa 1900.

Maps 197. d. 19, no. 5

As the supposed abode of gods, saints or monsters, the Alps had been objects of superstition and of religious veneration since the earliest times and their beauty had been admired, their slopes climbed, and their flora and fauna studied by Swiss scholars, such as Konrad Gesner (II.5.2), since at least the mid-sixteenth century. For most travellers, however, they were primarily regarded as major, unpleasant and rather ugly obstacles on their road to or from Italy. Although Swiss towns were regularly described in considerable detail, particularly by religious exiles and diplomats residing in Switzerland, only rarely did the countryside get more than a passing mention. Published descriptions by travellers, like Thomas Coryate (1610) or Gilbert Burnet (1686), and by ambassadors such as Giovanni della Torre (1607) or Abraham Stanyan (1714), moreover focused as much on the history, constitution, legal system, economy and politics of the cantons and on the customs of the people as on the noteworthy sights.

It was only after 1700, with the spread of a more rigorous scientific interest in geology and botany among the educated, inspired by Johann Jacob Scheuchzer (II.5.6) and, above all, with the awakening of Romanticism, under the influence of the writings of Rousseau (II.5.7,8) that the Alps became popular objects of interest in their own right, giving rise among most who contemplated them to satisfyingly fashionable sentiments of awe, fear and mystery. The traditions of Swiss liberty and the people's reputation for honesty, protestantism, industry, gallantry, cleanliness and simplicity added to the Romantic allure. The Genevois scientist, Horace-Bénédict de Saussure, and English writers, notably William Coxe, played a large part in popularising Switzerland among the leisured classes throughout Europe. Landscape artists from all over Europe, following the example of Swiss artists such as Aberli, also contributed through watercolours and prints to familiarising distant peoples with a Romantic image of the Alpine landscape.

View of the Grindelwald glacier engraved 'under the direction of [Joseph] Vernet, Painter to the King' in Paris *circa* 1780. From the King's Topographical Collection.
8 Tab. c. 6.

From the 1830s Britain again took the lead in promoting Switzerland as a centre for mountaineering, sanatoria and quality hotels for the middle classes for whom, with the advent of the railways, the country now became more accessible. Tourism rapidly came to fill the gap in the Swiss economy left by the ending of mercenary service. Such well-known mountain resorts as Interlaken, St. Moritz and Mürren were developed with English tourists largely in mind after 1860. After 1900 Sir Henry Lunn (1859-1939) and his son Arnold (1888 - 1974), who is commemorated by a statue outside Mürren station, made Switzerland into the all-season tourist mecca of today by popularising downhill skiing and slalom.

III.4.31

II.4.1   *A Curious Traveller*

On 24 May 1608 an eccentric English courtier with a restless curiosity for travel set out on a pioneering Grand Tour of Europe which was to take in Switzerland. Thomas Coryate journeyed into Italy by way of Paris, Lyons and the then favoured route over Mont Cenis. Having reached Venice, Coryate set off on the return trip through Venetia, entering the Graubünden via the Valtelline and the Splugen pass in mid-August. He carried with him an introduction to the noted protestant minister and controversialist Rudolph Hospinian. Coryate also records with evident pride his encounters with Henry Bullinger (the nephew of the famous reformer) and the philologist and orientalist Gaspar Waser.

Evident too is Coryate's fascination with the more lurid side of crime and punishment: the various punishments inflicted upon offending inhabitants of Zurich are treated in some detail, though he was impressed at the honesty and law-abiding nature of most of the Swiss. Coryate's curiosity was all-embracing extending to the fertility of the soil around Zurich, its sights, women's plaits, men's fashions, the high quality of the food served in Swiss inns and what must be the first description, couched in terms of wonderment, of what today are called duvets. Included also is a thumbnail sketch of the tugs-of-war which comprise Zurich's early history:

Zurich from G. della Torre
Descriptio Helvetiae (1607)
[II.2.2]

II.4.1: Titlepage

'Many bitter brunts also this Citie hath often endured both before the time of the confederation and since, having been tossed to and fro from one Lord to another, as if shee had beene Dame Fortunes tennis ball. But at this day by the gracious indulgence of the heavenly powers, it enjoyeth great peace and a very halcedonian time with the rest of the Helveticall Cities under that happie league of union, being subject neither to King nor Kaysar' (pp. 389-90) (2F7 ʳ⁻ᵛ).

Coryate also provides what is probably the earliest retelling in English of the legend of William Tell: although well-known to the better educated, the legend would not achieve widespread popularity in the English-speaking world until the 19th century, after the publication of Schiller's play based on the story.

After leaving Zurich on 27th August, Coryate set off for Baden to visit the famed hot springs, then on to Basle (where he attended a lecture on Homer given at the University by Jakob Zwingler). During September Coryate journeyed through Germany and the Netherlands, before arriving back in London on 3 October 1608.

The publication which charts Coryate's extraordinary progress is embellished with a titlepage engraved by William Hole which includes a head-and-shoulders portrait of the author and eight other small illustrations of his adventures. These are variously explained in fifty-odd pages of not-so-eulogistic doggerel which Coryate commissioned from well over sixty authors including such English Renaissance luminaries as Jonson, Chapman, Donne, Campion and Drayton.

This luxuriously finished example of the book was presented by Coryate to the eldest son of James I, Henry, Prince of Wales, to whom he dedicated the book.

Thomas Coryate, *Coryats Crudities Hastily gobled vp in five Moneths trauells in . . . Rhetia commonly called the Grisons country, Heluetia alias Switzerland . . . newly digested in the hungry aire of Odcomb in the county of Somerset, & now dispersed to the nourishment of the trauelling members of this kingdome* (London: Printed by W.S. [William Stansby], 1610).   *G. 6750*

II.4.2

II.4.3

II.4.2. The Alps Portrayed

Detail from an engraved
view of the fortress at
Aarburg showing tourists
viewing and sketching,
circa 1790.
From King George III's
Topographical Collection.
K. Top. 85.56 ᵃ

In 1770 Henry Temple, second Viscount Palmerston (1739-1802), a cultivated nobleman much interested in the arts and the sciences, spent six summer weeks visiting the Alps. William Pars (1742-1782) was employed by him to create an objective and scientific visual record. The resulting watercolours, which were partly influenced by the work of contemporary Swiss artists, succeeded remarkably well in also conveying the scale and grandeur of the Alps. A group of seven watercolours which Pars exhibited at the Royal Academy in 1771 were among the first specifically Alpine views to be seen publicly in England and they were soon engraved to achieve a still wider circulation. Within a few years, the sight of a young English Lord with tutor, servants and an artist in train had become a commonplace in Switzerland and stimulated the beginnings of the hotel trade.

The Staubbach waterfall, with its delicate, lace-like spray, became particularly popular and was to be eulogised by Goethe, Byron and Wordsworth. George III must also have been impressed, since he soon acquired this replica of one of Pars's most lovely views for his topographical collections.

William Pars, *'The Cascade of Luterbrun in the Canton of Berne'* [i.e. The valley of Lauterbrunnen and the Staubbach] 1770 (?).
Watercolour, pen and grey ink over pencil.   K. Top. 85. 65. 2a

II.4.3 The First Ascent of Mont Blanc

Horace-Bénédict de Saussure (1740-1799), a professor at the university of Geneva, was famous in his own time as a botanist, geologist, traveller and mountaineer. In 1770 he had acted as guide to Lord Palmerston and William Pars on their tour of the Alps. This interest in the Alps in all their aspects was to culminate in the publication between 1779 and 1796 of the four volume *Voyages dans les Alpes*, the first widely circulated work to present a detailed, readable description of the Swiss Alps intended both for the tourist and for fellow-scientists. While at work on this, in 1786, de Saussure sponsored the first ascent of Mont Blanc, the highest peak in Europe which lies just outside Switzerland. A year later he climbed the mountain himself. This perspective view commemorates his feat. It is traditional in its pictorial rendering of the terrain, yet forward-looking in its use of schematized symbols to emphasise roads and towns. It established a pattern for portraying mountains, be it for climbers or skiers, that, like mountain climbing, endures to this day.

'Vue perspective de la Vallée de Chamouni du Mont Blanc et des montagnes adjacentes . . . ou l'on a indiqué la route qu'a tenue au mois d'Aout 1787 Mr. le Professeur de Saussure' (Basel: Chrétien de Mechel, 1790).   K. Top. 76.77a

II.4.4 *A Literary Portrait of Switzerland*

In 1779 William Coxe (1747-1828) was persuaded to publish, in revised form, the letters he had sent to a friend in England while touring Switzerland some four years earlier as tutor to Lord Herbert, the son of the Earl of Pembroke. *Sketches of the Natural, Civil and Political State of Swisserland* enjoyed immediate popularity in England and abroad in an expanded French translation by Louis François Ramond, Baron de Carbonnières. Ten years later, and after three further tours, in 1779, 1785 and 1787, Coxe republished the letters under a new title, much-amended, expanded into three volumes and now covering the whole of Switzerland. With its epistolary form, its concentration on Swiss constitutional, civic and legal history and institutions, its acceptance of traditional Swiss peasant stereotypes and its protestant bias, it stands in a tradition dating back to Gilbert Burnet's *Letters containing an account of what seem'd most remarkable in travelling thru' Switzerland* of 1686. Yet its breadth of description, which embraced language, flora and fauna, geology and popular customs, its detailed coverage of the whole country, its interest in contemporary Swiss intellectual life and its thoroughness and accuracy, based on extensive reading, set it in a different class from its predecessors. The text is moreover plentifully enlivened with anecdotes to attract the casual reader. It was rapidly accepted as the standard description of the country and went through numerous English and foreign editions before 1809. This copy was published in Basle in 1802, just before a brief lull in the Napoleonic wars enabled English tourists to revisit Switzerland. The British Library possesses the notebook kept by Coxe during his Swiss and Italian tour of 1785.

William Coxe, *Travels in Switzerland in a series of letters to William Melmoth Esq.* (Basel: James Decker, 1802).   1048.g.17

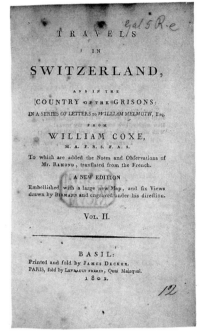

II.4.4

II.4.5 *Middle Class Tourism*

The modern guidebook evolved in the years after 1815. Made physically and financially for the pocket of the middle-class traveller, it provided the ready, practical up-to-date information about transport, inns, prices and possible routes that earlier, wealthier and more leisured visitors had had no need to concern themselves with. Murray's *Handbook* was of particular importance because, in its succeeding, revised editions, it became the standard Victorian guidebook to Switzerland. Murray researched the Swiss sections himself. Imbued with the confident, insular arrogance characteristic of his English contemporaries, his text abounds with trenchantly expressed tips for travellers. He had no truck with the traditional, sentimental view of the Swiss character and warned early on that 'A spirit of time-serving and a love of money appear the influencing motives in the national character, and the people who have enjoyed freedom longer than any other in Europe, are principally distinguished for fighting the battles of any master, ... for sending forth the most obsequious and drudging of valets; for extortionate innkeepers and, among the lower classes . . . for almost universal mendicity' (pp. xxx-xxxi).

John Murray III, *A Handbook for Travellers in Switzerland and the Alps of Savoy and Piedmont , including the Protestant valleys of the Waldenses.* (London, 1838).   10028.b.7

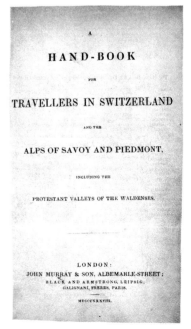

II.4.5

II.4.6 The New Tourist

George Scharf (1820-1895), the son of a middle-class German immigrant artist, was very different from the grand tourists whom Pars and Coxe had accompanied. He drew these sketches of the Place du Molard in Geneva and of the Genevois in his travel diary on 2 November 1839, while making his leisurely way to Asia Minor to act as draughtsman to an archaeological expedition sent out by the British Museum. He may well have utilised Murray's freshly-published *Handbook* to make the most of his limited time in Switzerland.

George Scharf the younger, [view of Place du Molard, Geneva], 1839.   *Add. MS 36488 A ff. 14v-15*

II.4.6

II.4.7 Lauterbrunnen Transformed

This photograph, from a turn of the century album, was taken from the same angle as the watercolour by Pars, but from the opposite side of the valley. Where in 1838 Murray recorded only one inn, the Capricorn [Steinbock], which he judged to be 'tolerably good', the 1904 edition records a further six well-established hotels, three of which merited stars, with Anglican services being held every Sunday in the Steinbock, nearest the station. All are to be seen on this photograph, together with the railway which had brought this much-praised spot within easy reach of innumerable English tourists. Some, however, still sought the older, simpler Switzerland higher up in the mountains or, as with Samuel Butler, in the then little-known valleys of Italian Switzerland, immortalised in his *Alps and Sanctuaries* of 1881.

Wehrli & Kilchberg, Zurich: Photograph of Lauterbrunnen and the Staubbach, c.1900.
Maps 197. d. 19 no. 12.

II.4.7

II.4.8 *Tragedy on the Matterhorn*

Petrarch is known to have climbed mountains in the fourteenth century, but the father of modern mountaineering, of climbing peaks for pleasure rather than for scientific purposes, was a Swiss, Fr. Placidus of Disentis in Graubünden, who scaled eight virgin peaks between 1788 and 1824. It was peace in Europe after 1815 and growing British prosperity which helped to set the scene for what came to be known as the golden age of mountaineering.

Edward Whymper (1840-1911), an artist and journalist, was influenced by this new spirit, and with others of his countrymen, spurred by the vision of beauty and the prospect of a contest with nature, developed the sport and craft of conquering the rock peaks, and founded the exclusive Alpine Club in 1854. It is Whymper's ascent of the Matterhorn that fired the popular imagination with its combination of triumph and tragedy, the mysterious vision of the three crosses after the fatal accident, and the record of the climb first in a letter to *The Times* and then in *Scrambles amongst the Alps*. Whymper had attempted

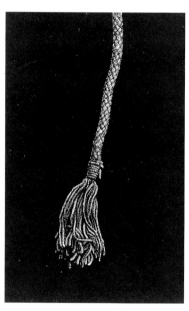

The rope that caused
the disaster.
From Edward Whymper,
*Scrambles amongst the Alps
in the years 1860-1869*
(4th ed., London,
Edinburgh, 1893).
K.T.C. 11. a. 4.

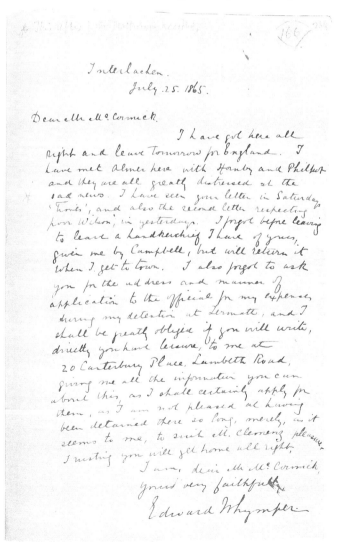

Letter from Edward Whymper to - McCormack, Interlaken, 25th July 1865, mentioning the 'sad news' and his consequent internment in Zermatt. From the Blakeney Papers.

Add. MS 63090 no. 166

the peak seven times before, but on 14 July 1865 triumph seemed assured when a united party of Whymper with Lord Francis Douglas and his guides, the older and younger Peter Taugwalder, and Charles Hudson with his protegé Douglas Hadow and the senior guide Michel Croz, saw off an Italian attempt and reached the summit. The circumstances of the disaster that followed remain controversial. It is known that Croz was leading the party, helping the inexperienced Hadow, when Hadow slipped, causing Croz, Douglas and Hudson to fall: between Douglas and the elder Taugwalder was only the thinnest of the three ropes the expedition had taken. It snapped - as shown in the illustration – and the four slid and fell down the precipices to their deaths 4000 feet beneath. It was later suggested that Whymper had cut one of the good ropes in his determination to reach the summit, compelling the use of inferior quality ropes on the descent. As leader of the expedition, he was interned on his return to Zermatt, as he angrily reflects in the letter, 'merely, as it seems to me, to suit M. Clemenz [the president of the court of enquiry's] pleasure'. Although the investigation established that there had been no foul play, Whymper never recovered to climb in the Alps again, and mountaineering suffered considerable adverse comment. The elder Taugwalder was accused, unjustly, of contributing towards the disaster through his desire for self-preservation and was hounded out of Switzerland. Whymper did little to defend him. The younger Taugwalder, however, became ever more experienced and the annotation on the photograph of him with his family in 1920 states that he ascended the Matterhorn 125 times – the apprentices had themselves become the masters. After the initial set-back, the Alpine Club continued its activities with W.A. Coolidge as its leading light and the maverick A.F. Mummery bringing a new joie de vivre into the sport.

Photograph of P. Taugwalder (junior) and family, 1920 in front of alpine hut 'ascended Matterhorn 125 times'

Add. MS 63141

II.5   *Swiss Enterprise*

Zurich Taler of 1736
showing the town
viewed from the lake.
(slightly reduced)
[III.3.55]

'In Italy for thirty years under the Borgias they had warfare, terror, murder, bloodshed but they produced Michelangelo, Leonardo da Vinci and the Renaissance. In Switzerland they had brotherly love, they had five hundred years of democracy and peace and what did that produce – the cuckoo clock' [Orson Welles as Harry Lime in the film, *The Third Man*]

II.5.4: detail showing Basle and the Rhine.

Circle of
Daniel Lindtmayer,
The arms of Chur
from G. della Torre,
Descriptio Helvetiae (1607)
[II.2.2]

Contrary to the words that Orson Welles put into the mouth of Harry Lime, Switzerland has had no more internal peace, democracy and brotherly love than other nations, while the cuckoo clock originated in the German Black Forest. On the other hand, Rousseau and Jung, Borromini and Le Corbusier, Klee and Giacometti were Swiss, Holbein and Einstein regarded themselves as Swiss and the first modern botanist and zoologist was Swiss. But all this is not immediately obvious since, despite the presence of many notable authors, artists, architects, craftsmen and philosophers, the cultures of French and Italian-speaking Switzerland have tended to merge with those of France and Italy, or, more precisely that of the areas, such as Lombardy in the case of Ticino, of which they culturally and geographically form a part. The culture of the largest group in Switzerland, the German Swiss forming nearly three-

Silver-cased chaise watch
shown with its outer,
leather protective case.
Jean-Baptiste Duboulle.
Geneva, 1650.
B.M. 1888, 12-1.22
Reproduced by courtesy of
the Trustees of the
British Museum.

quarters of the population, has been better able to make its distinctive presence felt through the work of authors such as Gottfried Keller, the historian Jakob Burckhardt, and the playwright Friedrich Dürrenmatt. Just as distinctly 'Swiss' are the numerous doctors, mathematicians and naturalists from Paracelsus and Gesner in the sixteenth century to Saussure, Scheuchzer, Albrecht von Haller, the Bernouillis and Euler, in the eighteenth when French and German Switzerland contained some of the liveliest centres of the European Enlightenment. Swiss cartography has been pre-eminent since before 1500, as has its topographical art, seen as much on coins and medals as in engravings, drawings and watercolours. Swiss humanitarianism can be seen before Dunant in the theories of the educationalist Heinrich Pestalozzi of Zurich and more recently in the work of Carl Jung.

Swiss culture has long been tied to the twin concepts of efficiency and technical excellence, be it as watchmakers, bankers, chefs or restaurateurs. These have undoubtedly helped to create the prosperity that is so evident in

Detail from the 'Dufour' map of Switzerland, created 1842-64, showing the Jungfrau and surrounding mountains and valleys.

the Switzerland of today, but they have also contributed not a little towards the equally evident Swiss tendency towards blandness, materialism, smugness and conservatism. These have stirred many contemporary Swiss artists, writers and film makers, following the lead of Max Frisch, into revolt against traditional Swiss procedures, institutions, assumptions, and beliefs, including the whole notion of celebrating national anniversaries. But this very revolt reveals the continuing vitality of Switzerland's cultural life.

II.5.1 *The First Dated Book Printed in Switzerland*

Although generally accepted that at least three books had been printed at Basle before the printers' strike of late 1471, the earliest unequivocal date that can be associated with printing in Switzerland is the Vigil of St. Martin [10 November] 1470, which appears in the colophon concluding the *Mamotrectus super Bibliam* printed by canon Helias Helyae at Beromünster some seventeen years after the introduction of printing at Mainz by Gutenberg but five years before the first book printed in England. Peter Schoeffer's Mainz edition of the *Mamotrectus* bears the same date in the colophon, apparently coincidentally, as the notion that Helyae's edition was reprinted from Schoeffer's is disproved by a copy of his edition now preserved in Lucerne which was bought on 27 November 1470 for three gulden.

The *Mamotrectus*, of which this is thus a joint first edition, is a basic handbook for priests explaining difficult words in the Bible, Breviary and Homilies and giving simple guidance on interpretation, and was compiled by the Franciscan Johannes Marchesinus of Reggio Emilia towards the end of the thirteenth

II.5.1: the colophon

century. Its utility and popularity are well attested by the numerous manuscript and printed copies that survive. It earned the opprobrium of the reformers, however, being characterised by Martin Luther as 'Münchenmist und Teufelsdreck' ('monkish dung and devil's shit'), and it was not reprinted thereafter.

Helyae was no youthful enthusiast for technology when he embarked on his venture: presented to his canonry in 1419 and matriculated at Heidelberg university in 1422, he must have been nearly seventy when he became involved in printing. He introduced a distinctive and curious gothic type for the *Mamotrectus*, only used once again in his undated *Psalterium cum canticis*, moving to a roman typeface (the first to be used in Switzerland), for four further books, the last being dated 30 July 1473. Helyae died on 20 March 1475, and his press was not revived. Only at Basle was printing in modern Switzerland to continue through the 1470s (apart from the short-lived press at Burgdorf), until Adam Steinschaber opened the first press at Geneva in 1478. The early Basle presses too maintained a steady production of the practical works aimed at a largely ecclesiastical market that characterise Helyae's output, and place him firmly in the early Swiss printing tradition.

Johannes Marchesinus, *Mamotrectus Super Bibliam* (Beromünster 'in pago Ergowie': Helyas Helyae de Lauffen, 10 November 1470). *C.10. c.12.*

II.5.2 *A First in Zoology*

Konrad Gesner *Icones animalium* (Zurich: Christof Froschouer, 1553). *459. c. 9(1)*

Konrad Gesner of Zurich (1516-1565) was one of the founders of modern zoology and bibliography. He was also town physician of Zurich, a naturalist, gardener, professor of Greek at Lausanne, linguist, author of 72 books, an early lover of mountains, and a pioneer of mountaineering, who scaled the Pilatus near Lucerne in 1555. A passionate cataloguer and classifier, his *Bibliotheca Universalis* (1545), was the first critical bibliography, listing and evaluating the works of about 1800 Latin, Greek and Hebrew authors. He is best known, however, for his *Historiae animalium* (1551-8, 1587) which represented the first modern attempt to classify all recorded animal life and (not entirely successfully) to distinguish observed facts from the myths inherited from the middle ages. The numerous woodcut illustrations in the five volumes, on quadrupeds that bear their young, quadrupeds that lay eggs, birds, fishes and aquatic animals and serpents, were not mere decoration. They were intended to establish the accuracy of his data. Many were copied from earlier books, illustrated by artists such as Dürer, but some, such as the chamois standing before some Alpine peaks, seem to be based on Gesner's own observations during his excursions in the mountains. Gesner's plan to classify plant life was cut short by his death from the plague, but he left about 1,500 woodcuts of plants, flowers and seeds.

II.5.3 *A Master Mathematician and Clockmaker*

Jost Bürgi (1552-1632), from Lichtensteig in St. Gallen, was a pioneering mathematician, instrument-maker, clockmaker and inventor. As was the case with so many talented Swiss, opportunities were lacking in his homeland and he took service abroad with the Landgrave of Hesse and, for a period after 1604, with the Emperors Rudolf II and Matthias in Prague. Independently of his Scottish contemporary, John Napier, he invented what were substantially logarithms and he also anticipated Galileo and Huygens in discovering that a clock could be regulated by a pendulum.

II.5.3

His skills as an author, however, were not on a par with his others. In 1592 he commissioned the engraver Anton Eisenhoit to produce a frontispiece for a book in which he intended to advertise the numerous ways in which a geometrical triangulation instrument that he had created could be used. The design shows his pendulum clock and several scientific instruments made by Bürgi as well as illustrating the theme of the forthcoming work. In 1619 the portrait of the now 67-year-old Bürgi was added by Aegidius Sadeler, but he never finished his book, which was only finally completed and published in 1648 by his brother-in-law.

In the following centuries, Switzerland was to nurture an impressive number of major mathematicians, most notably Leonhard Euler, and no less than five members of the Bernouilli family of Basle, most of whom worked abroad for much of their lives and corresponded with their English counterparts. As a result the British Library possesses many of their letters as well as their published works.

III.4.32

Benjamin Bramer, *Apollonius Cattus* (3rd edition; Kassel, 1684).   *8535.c.5*

II.5.4 *A Tribute to His Home Town*

This bird's-eye view of Basle from the North is an outstanding example of the town views on paper (and on coins and medals) in which the Germans and the German Swiss excelled between about 1550 and 1800. Its maker, Matthäus Merian (1593-1650), came of a distinguished Basle family and was perhaps the greatest topographer of his time. The view was created and printed in the spring of 1615, following the completion of his artistic training in Paris, and Merian himself, probably assisted by some existing plans, did the extensive preliminary surveying. Although the streets are slightly widened so as to show the facades of the buildings, and a very few trifling errors have been noted, the view is astoundingly topographically accurate. Yet it is primarily a celebration of Switzerland's most prosperous city and its government.

II.5.4: Detail

Basle is shown secure and happy, dominated by its great Münster (3) and churches such as the Barfüsskirche (now the historical museum) (11), surrounded by orderly gardens and vineyards and protected by strong, well-guarded fortifications and ditches filled with deer. Waggons and barges bring supplies to the City, the streets are clean and replete with fountains and fishing takes place on the Rhine. The ornate cartouche contains a graceful dedication to the City fathers and burgesses, who are depicted, well-dressed and well-fed in the foreground (on a site now occupied by Swiss pharmaceutical factories). Triumphing angels support the City's arms, while boats and the gate near the Albankirche (7) fire their guns in well-deserved salute.

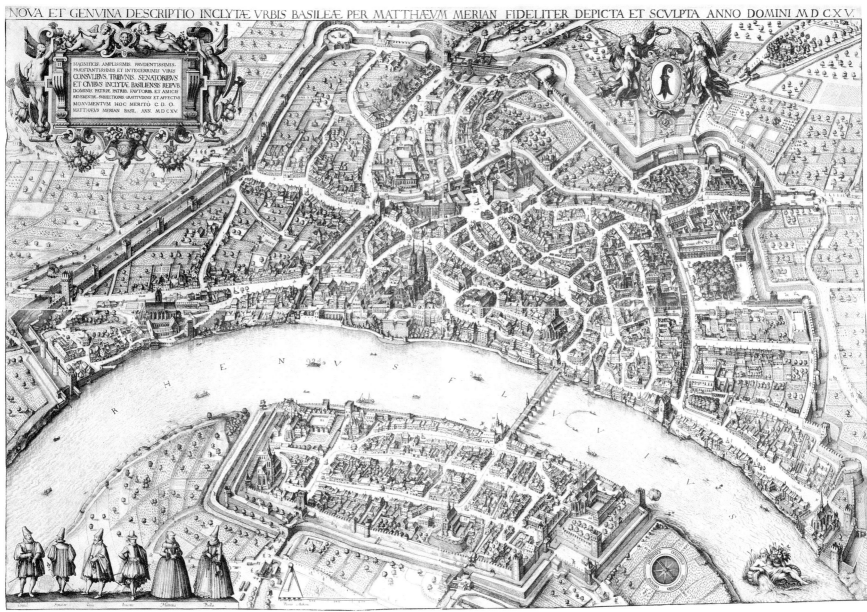

II.5.4

Merian was awarded 59 gulden by the authorities for a related drawing on 6 May 1615. But he was not to make his career in Basle. By the autumn, and before he could prepare the explanatory text, which followed in 1617, he had left the City and was to spend most of the rest of his life in Frankfurt at the head of a publishing firm that survived into the next century.

Matthäus Merian, *Nova et genvina descriptio inclytae vrbis Basileae per Matthaevm Merian fideliter depicta et scvlpta anno domini MDCXV*. Engraving 70.5 x 105.5 cm.   K. Top. 85.49

II.5.5   *Home in the Mendrisiotto*

II.5.5

Pier Francesco Mola (1612-66) came from the village of Coldrerio or, in dialect (and on the Scheuchzer map), Coldré not far from Como on the Swiss-Italian border. His father worked as an architect in Rome and one of the leading medallists working in Italy in the earlier seventeenth century, Gaspare Mola (c. 1580 - 1640), was probably a cousin. Despite his congenital laziness, Pier Francesco became an artist of some standing in Rome where, after 1650, he enjoyed the patronage of leading families such as the Chigi and Pamphili. An individualistic painter, he had contacts with Poussin and Cortona.

This sketch was made during a visit to his home village in 1642, probably while enjoying the sun in the walled enclosure (or, in dialect, 'Cios') behind his house. The notes in dialect, which he added to the drawing, explain that he was looking westwards over the fertile plain of the Mendrisiotto with the church of S. Antonio in Genestrerio ('genestre') in the middle distance with the Monti di Santa Maria and Brusata on the left and the mountains at the south-western end of Lake Lugano on the horizon. The main focus of Mola's attention, however, was an old apple tree which, as he records on its trunk, stood ten (feet?) 'nel nostro Cios'. ['within our enclosure'].

Medal by Gaspare Mola showing Vincenzo Gonzaga, Duke of Mantua (1587-1612), and, on the reverse, St. George and the dragon. (80% of actual size)
[III.3.49]

Numerous architects, artists, sculptors and craftsmen stemmed from the southern part of the modern canton Ticino, and particularly the villages on or near Lake Lugano. The best-known are Carlo Maderno (1556-1629) who designed the facade of St. Peter's, his kinsman Francesco Borromini (1599-1667), the architect of some of Rome's most impressive Baroque churches, and the short-lived Caravaggesque painter, Giovanni Serodine (1600-1630). However, craftsmen from the area also created the mosaic pavements before the high altar of Westminster Abbey in the thirteenth century, while Artari and Bagutti were responsible for the plasterwork in numerous eighteenth century English country houses and churches such as St. Martin's in the Fields in London. Ticinese architects, in the persons of Pietro Antonio Solario (c.1450-93) and Domenico Trezzini (1670-1734), were active in creating the walls and towers of the Kremlin in the fifteenth century and in building St. Petersburg three hundred years later. Nor is the impulse extinguished as the work of the acclaimed, if controversial, modern Ticinese architect, Mario Botta, demonstrates.

Pier Francesco Mola (1612-1666), *Landscape near Coldrerio with apple tree*, 1642
Pen, brown ink and wash. 28.5 x 21 cm.   B.M. 1898-12-16-1

II.5.6 *Nature on the Map*

II.5.6: detail showing building of the
'Devil's Bridge'.

Johann Jacob Scheuchzer of Zurich (1672-1733), a physician, mathematician, naturalist, ethnographer, and a leading figure in the early Swiss Enlightenment, was responsible for the creation between 1708 and 1712 of the best eighteenth century map of Switzerland. Scheuchzer, who had very close links with England, constructed his map around the routes of the nine journeys he had made through the Alps between 1702 and 1711. His interests are reflected in the decoration surrounding the map where depictions by Johann Melchior Füssli of scenes in the Alps (e.g. the Rhone Glacier [bottom left]) and countryside (e.g. Rheinfall near Schaffhausen [top of right side]), of natural disasters (bottom right), natural phenomena such as rainbows at the foot of waterfalls (bottom left), of stones and fossils he had discovered (top of right side) and of countryside pursuits such as cheese-making (top centre), replace the town views and fashion plates that had previously been standard.

II.5.6

Scheuchzer was aware of the possibilities of scientific measurement but was not sufficiently skilled to practise it. His map is, nevertheless, the first to give altitudes for mountains. It also includes many new placenames and much religious-political and military information: its publication followed the conclusion of a religious civil war. Old legends still survive, however, and together with the Dragon of Lucerne (bottom centre), the Devil, under the supervision of a monk, can be seen under the cartouche at the top left, constructing the 'Devil's Bridge' over the Schöllenen gorge which after about 1220 had made the Gotthard Pass practicable for commercial traffic.

Since the creation of the first modern map by Conrad Türst in 1498, the Swiss have been consistently amongst the very best mapmakers in Europe. Today's official mapping is renowned for its impressive semi-pictorial rendering of mountains, and General Guillaume-Henri Dufour, a founding father of the modern Swiss state in 1847-8, was also responsible for one of the great achievements of nineteenth century cartography: the large-scale mapping of the whole of Switzerland between 1842 and 1864.

J.J. Scheuchzer. *'Nova Helvetiae Tabula Geographica'*, (Zurich,1713). 4 sheets. 110 x 148 cm. Scale ca. 1:230,000.
24405 (12)

II.5.7 *Rousseau on Rousseau*

The son of a Genevan watchmaker, Jean-Jacques Rousseau (1712-1778) left his native city at the age of sixteen, subsequently leading a peripatetic, restless existence in France, Italy, Switzerland and England where he took refuge in 1766-7 after the French and Genevese authorities banned two of his works for their political radicalism and critique of Christianity. An outsider in French society, Rousseau's sense of isolation was compounded by temperamental and ideological clashes with his former friends in the Enlightenment such as Voltaire and his final years were dominated by his dread of a conspiracy against him, which was in part well-founded, but partly also a product of growing paranoia.

II.5.7

Rousseau, whose pride in his homeland and its values may be seen as a dominant factor in his life and works, was one of the most influential writers of the age. His political theories influenced leaders of the French Revolution while his autobiographical and fictional writings helped to shape the pre-Romantic sensibility, an aspect of which was an enhanced awareness of the awesome majesty of mountains.

This is one of four autograph fair copies of the first of three autobiographical dialogues known collectively as *'Rousseau juge de Jean-Jacques'* from the title page of this manuscript. Rousseau composed them between 1772-76 as an apologia for his life and works, which he felt were being deliberately misrepresented by members of the 'conspiracy' against him. Fearing that this work would be tampered with or destroyed, on 6 April 1776 Rousseau entrusted this copy of the first dialogue to Brooke Boothby, a young English visitor, who had been a neighbour of his during his exile in England. Directly he had relinquished this copy, Rousseau became convinced that Boothby was in league with members of the 'conspiracy'. However, after Rousseau's death in 1778, Boothby published this manuscript at Lichfield in 1780 (the earliest edition of the first dialogue), presenting it to the British Museum in January 1781.

J.J. Rousseau, *'Rousseau juge de Jean-Jacques'*, 1776. Autograph fair copy   *Add. MS 4925*

II.5.8   *Rousseau's Island*

Following their publication in 1762, two of the philosopher's major works, *Emile* and the *Social Contract*, were condemned by the authorities – the former in France, and both in his native Geneva. Rousseau became a fugitive and a wanderer, shunned for his unorthodox religious views.

In 1765, after an attack on his home by an angry mob at Môtiers in the Jura, he took refuge on the Île de Saint-Pierre in the Lake of Bienne (Biel). The whole island belonged to the Burgerspital of Berne, and its only dwelling was occupied by an official of the hospital and his household.

In the posthumously published *Rêveries du promeneur solitaire*, Rousseau describes his manner of life on the island. Apart from studying wild flowers and helping his hosts with the apple harvest, most of his time seems to have been given over to the joys of 'dolce far niente'. One of his favourite occupations was to drift across the lake in a rowing boat, lying on his back and gazing up at the sky; another to sit by the shore at evening, lulled into a kind of trance by the regular sound and movement of the waves.

This happy interlude was not to last, however; after six weeks the Bernese authorities expelled Rousseau from the island without explanation. He

II.5.8

afterwards wrote that no place on earth had made him so happy or left him with such deep nostalgia.

Because of the links between Rousseau, Romanticism and the growth of English interest in the Alps, numerous prints of 'Rousseau's Island' were published in England. This is one of the most accomplished and comes from King George III's Topographical Collection, which is notable for the number and quality of it views.

'2nd View of the Island of St. Peter on the Lake of Bienne in Swisserland. The residence of JJ Rousseau Anno 1765'. 'King sculp'. Hand-coloured engraving.   *K. Top. 85. 69b*

II.5.9 *Geneva the Banking Centre*

Proximity to France, making Geneva a convenient tax-haven and providing the French government and also its enemies with a source of funds, lay behind the city's emergence as a banking centre in the late 17th century. The founding of its stock exchange in 1850 - long before those of Basle or Zurich – encouraged this international outlook.

It is not surprising, then, that Geneva appears as the European centre for the American Joint-National Bank on this map compiled by Charles Bowles in 1871. Bowles, an American banker, was using the map to advocate his plan for speeding up the international circulation of U.S. government funds by using the latest communication technology, telegraphy. The red circles on the map show the straight-line distances from Geneva to financial centres in Europe and beyond. For purposes of comparison, the tables at the left also give road distances in miles and mail distances in miles and hours.

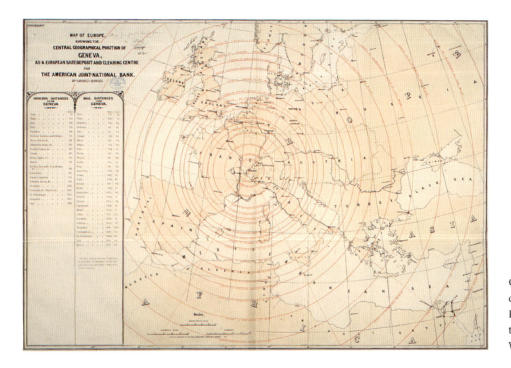

Charles Bowles, 'Map of Europe showing the central geographical position of Geneva as a European safe-deposit and clearing centre for the American Joint-National Bank' ([London]: Whiteman and Bass, 1871).   *1035. (42)*

II.5.10 *Precision Engineering and the Micro-gramophone*

Probably the smallest working gramophone ever, the Mikiphone arrived on the British market in 1926. It was patented by N. and A. Vadasz in 1924. When folded away in its nickel-plated case, the gramophone resembles a large pocket watch – perhaps predictably since it seems that the workmen who produced it had formerly been watchmakers. Records of up to ten inches (25.4 cm) in diameter can be played, clamped to the spindle, as they greatly overhang the turn-table. Instead of a horn, a plastic resonator, attached directly to the soundbox, gives some amplification.

Typically for a Swiss product it is well engineered. Swiss-made components were often used in acoustic gramophones assembled in Britain and elsewhere. Paillard motors were popular. Thorens made cylinder phonograms as early as 1904 and supply hi-fi turntables to this day.

Mikiphone   *NSA 19 Frow 1988*

II.5.10

II.5.11 *Analytical Psychology*

Carl Gustav Jung (1875-1961) was born in Basle and worked in Switzerland for most of his life. He was one of the three leading exponents of the theory of psychoanalysis, along with Freud and Adler. In 1912 however he broke with Freud, and went on to develop his own system of 'analytical psychology' with its centre in Zurich.

In 1986 the British Library acquired 50 volumes of unpublished lecture notes taken down mainly by his English-speaking students between 1925 and 1941. Several volumes deal with dream analysis. As a child, Jung had experienced extraordinarily vivid dreams, and the interpretation of dreams was to play a major part in his psychological theories (as it did in those of Freud) and in his practice of psychotherapy.

Central to his theories was that of the 'collective unconscious'. He believed that the individual's subconscious mind was formed not only by personal experiences, but also from inherited notions known as 'archetypes' which originated in the primitive history of mankind and are still common to all people, whatever their cultural background. Only by taking these historical factors into account was he able to give a satisfactory explanation of his own patients' dreams.

II.5.11

Carl Jung *Dream Analysis Vol. 1. Notes on the seminar in analytical psychology given by Dr. C. G. Jung. Zurich Autumn 1928. New edition 1938.*   *Cup. 409. b. 14*

II.6 *The British and the Swiss*

Anglo-Swiss relations have almost invariably been extremely friendly. Their basis has, however, varied considerably over the centuries. For much of the time, be it in 1516, during the Italian Wars, in 1707 during the wars against Louis XIV, during the 1790s at the time of the French Revolution, during the Second World War, or even, in much modified form, today, it has been based on certain shared cultural values and a common apprehension of one or other of Switzerland's and Britain's powerful neighbours. For the two centuries after 1530, religion created bonds between England, Scotland and Switzerland's numerous protestant cantons, and Swiss precepts were very influential in the formative years of Anglicanism and Scottish Presbyterianism. In the eighteenth century an Enlightened perception of their shared 'liberty' tended to unite the ruling classes of the two countries while the work of Swiss landscape artists such as Johann Ludwig Aberli (1723-1786) and Louis Ducros (1748-1810), inspired several of the leading English watercolourists. Since about 1770, the allure of mountains, lakes, sanatoria and hotels has made innumerable Britons firm friends of and very effective propagandists for a country where they have spent so many of their happiest and most relaxed hours: few more so than Winston Churchill, who spent his honeymoon in Riederalp in Valais.

Indeed it is perhaps the personal links that have counted most of all: be they the sixteenth-century English and Scottish religious refugees, eighteenth century Englishmen like Gibbon who literally lost their hearts in Switzerland, nineteenth century City businessmen who financed the creation of much of the Swiss rail network and others who founded some of Switzerland's great firms, such as Brown Boveri, or philanthropists like Montagu Montagu (1786-1863) who founded a still-existing old-people's home in La Neuveville by Lake Biel. Nor should the artists be forgotten, most notably Turner, who repeatedly visited and depicted the Alps, and in this century, Ben Nicolson, who spent many of his most creative years in the Ticino. The links have not been one-sided, however, for there have been many Swiss – diplomats, artists, medallists, watchmakers, bankers and restauranteurs – who made their homes in and their mark on Britain, often centuries ago, and adopted British nationality, without losing their links with their homeland, or even, in very many cases, their Swiss nationality.

J. L. Aberli, View of Nidau
near Lake Bienne (Biel),
c.1770.
From King George III's
Topographical Collection.
K.Top. 85. 55-c-1.

The opening lines of
Edward Gibbon's
unfinished history of
Switzerland, the
*Introduction à l'histoire
Générale de la
République des Suisses.*
Add. MS 34881, f. 170

II.6.1 *Not up to Genevan Standards!*

Edward VI (1547-1553) was the first protestant king of England and he and his council naturally looked to the various Reformed churches on the continent for a successful working model. This they found in particular in John Calvin's Geneva. Calvin (1509-1564), seeing the opportunity to advance the protestant cause, entered into correspondence with the priggish and precocious young king and also with his uncle Edward Seymour, Duke of Somerset and Protector of the kingdom.

Medallic portrait of John Calvin, 1552. (75% of actual size)

III.3.78.

Letter of John Calvin to Edward Seymour, Duke of Somerset, Geneva 25 July 1551.

Add. MS 4277, f.45

In this letter to the Duke, written in French, in his own hand, Calvin, after thanking Somerset for his kind reception of his envoy, Nicolas des Gallars, later minister of the French congregation in London, reminds him of the need for an educated clergy committed to propagating the protestant faith. This indeed was one of the salient features of the Genevan Church. Accordingly, he strongly condemns the greed of those laymen who, having appropriated funds confiscated from monasteries and chantries, fail to use them to make adequate financial provision for the clergy in their own parishes, thus 'defrauding God's people of their spiritual nourishment'. Ironically the Duke of Somerset had himself made a fortune out of church lands and wealth, but in Geneva the King and his uncle are still commemorated for their protestant sympathies.

II.6.2 *The Geneva Bible*

The Geneva New Testament (1557) and the Geneva Bible were translated and published by William Whittingham and other English protestant refugees from Queen Mary's persecutions who had settled in Geneva. In Geneva 'the store of heavenly learning and judgement; the place where God hath appointed us to dwell', lived Theodore Beza, the greatest biblical scholar of his day, who had done much to establish the text. There, too, the French Bible was being revised and improved. Although large folio bibles in English had long been available in English churches for consultation and public reading, the people could not take them home. The Geneva Bible, however, was published in a handy cheap quarto format for private study. It is a compact presentation of a long text, incorporating marginal notes and variants, headnotes to each page, summaries of each book and chapter, together with illustrations and maps. It was the first English bible to be divided into numbered verses, which make quotation and reference easier but tends to break the continuity of the narrative. It was also the first English bible to be printed in a 'black letter', not roman, type.

Whittingham took Tyndale's version as his basic text for the New Testament (1557) and revised it 'by the most approved Greek examples and . . . translations in other tongues'. Additional words not found in the Greek but required by English idioms were for the first time distinguished and printed in italics.

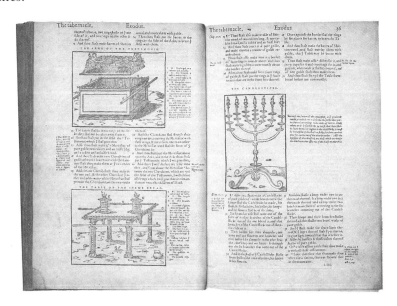

The Geneva Bible, easily the most accurate English translation before the Authorised Version (1611), was the first to be made throughout from the languages in which the Bible was originally written. It remained in successive editions, printed at first in Geneva and then in England, the household bible of the English-speaking protestant world for three generations.

The Bible and Holy Scriptures conteyned in the Olde and New Testaments. Translated according to the Ebrue and Greke, and conferred with the best translations in divers languages. With the most profitable annotations upon all the hard places etc. (Geneva: Rowland Hall, 1560).

II.6.3 *A Strategic Friendship*

Unopened letters of Deputies of Grisons and of the protestant deputies to Duke of Marlborough, Chur, 24 November/ 5 December 1707. *Add. Ch. 76095.A and B.*

Letters rarely survive unopened for more than three and a half centuries. That these were not unsealed did not indicate indifference on Marlborough's part: Queen Anne's envoy in Switzerland, Abraham Stanyan, enclosed English translations when forwarding them to the Duke, who knew no German. In return for allowing Allied troops free passage through the Valtelline, one of the few valleys linking northern and southern Europe, the deputies of the Grisons or Graubünden asked for English support in their dispute with Milan which was controlled by the Austrian Habsburgs. The letter from the protestant deputies reinforced the request by pointing out the advantages that would follow for protestants in the Valtelline. Strategic and religious considerations were more than sufficient for the Duke who, as his surviving maps show, was acutely aware of the importance of the Valtelline to the Allied war effort. English pressure was soon being applied in Vienna.

The three seals on the better addressed letter are those of the League of Ten Jurisdictions, the God's House League and the Grey (or Upper) League, which collectively constituted the Graubünden or Grisons. Since 1512, though scarcely able to agree among themselves about anything, they had exercised joint sovereignty over the Valtelline. Such feeble control, by ostensible neutrals over one of the poorest but militarily most important areas of Europe, provoked innumerable international crises and internal friction until 1797, when Napoleon removed the valley from the jurisdiction of the Graubünden.

II.6.4 *An Englishman on the Swiss*

Abraham Stanyan (1669(?)-1732) served as Queen Anne's representative to the Swiss cantons, Geneva and the Graubünden from 1705 to 1714. There his duties involved countering French intrigues, obtaining free passage for Allied troops through the Valtelline and ensuring that Allied armies were properly financed. This entailed much travel during which he got to know the country intimately. He composed his *Account of Switzerland* on his return, motivated by the intense ignorance of the country in England and seeing in Switzerland a modern form of the much-admired states' system of ancient Greece. The *Account* takes the form of the 'Relation' that ambassadors customarily composed for the benefit of their successors and one chapter is devoted to 'the people and their dispositions'.

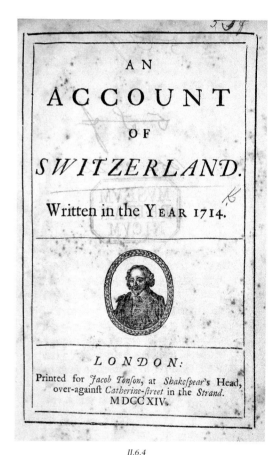

II.6.4

In 1714 the Swiss were the butts of what in England today would be called 'Irish' jokes and the existence or otherwise of Swiss wit was a subject for debate. Indeed, as Stanyan says, 'whoever undertakes to defend them upon that head is in danger of being thought to have a very little share of it himself.' Indeed so bad was the reputation that some 'especially those of Neufchatel and Geneva . . . look upon it as a real misfortune to be Switzers, and don't care to pass for such, but in case of need, that is when they want the protection of the cantons'. Nevertheless, Stanyan asserts that 'I have no where met with men of more . . . true wit and genuine humour than are to be found among some . . who have had the advantage of a good education improved by travel . . . The French, who laugh at the Switzers are generally out-witted by them, when they treat of any business'. The reputation for dullness was due to poor education, itself a consequence of the poverty of the country and its peoples: 'in short, they have more wit and perhaps less sincerity than the world allows them.... their virtues are natural to them and their vices chiefly owing to the temptation which men struggling with difficulties are apt to fall under'.

The book was first published anonymously when Switzerland was in the news following the outbreak of civil war in 1712 and the success of the protestant cantons. Its accuracy was soon recognised. Stanyan's authorship was acknowledged in later editions. It was translated into French and published in France and Switzerland, only finally being superseded by Archdeacon Coxe's writings in the 1770s.

Abraham Stanyan, *An Account of Switzerland written in the year 1714* (London: Jacob Tonson, 1714).

1054.c.22

II.6.5   *A Swiss on the English*

Béat Louis de Muralt (1665-1749), the scion of a patrician family from Berne, visited England in 1694 after completing his education in Geneva and serving in the French army. His *Lettres sur les Anglois* (translated into English as *Letters describing the character and customs of the English . . . nation*), consisting of six letters to an unnamed Swiss correspondent, were written during this visit, but were not published until 1725. As the English title makes clear, Muralt's main purpose was to explore the salient features of the English character. These he identified as being a love of liberty, independence of mind and good sense. A friendly, but not uncritical observer, however, Muralt, in common with other foreign visitors, comments adversely on the ferocity of the English, a characteristic reflected in the violent pastimes of the common people such as cock-fights, wrestling matches and football: 'a very troublesome and insolent [diversion] . . . where they take a great deal of pleasure in breaking windows and coach glasses'.

Muralt's *Lettres*, first published anonymously in Geneva at a time when England was challenging French political and cultural hegemony, aroused much interest and ran into many editions in France, Switzerland and Germany. The second edition of the English translation gives Muralt's name on the title-page. Muralt's work has been overshadowed by Voltaire's *Lettres philosphiques* (1734), based on a period of exile in England in 1726-8, which praised English institutions and thought the better to crticise French absolutism. Nevertheless, Muralt's book continued to be read alongside Voltaire's and found an attentive reader in Rousseau whose idea of the English people is based on the *Lettres sure les Anglois*. Muralt's praise of English commonsense at the expense of French frivolity in particular coincided with his, and other Swiss writers', view of the contrast between the Swiss and French character.

Louis Beat de Muralt, *Letters describing . . . the English & French Nations* (London, 1726).

10106.ee.6

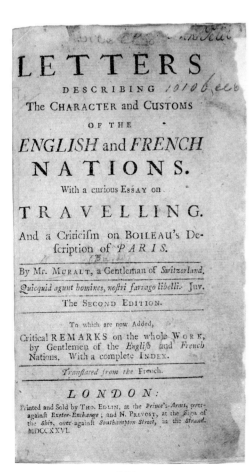

II.6.6

II.6.6. *In the Corridors of Power*

Before 1800, several Swiss nationals represented Britain abroad, ostensibly as envoys of the British kings as electors of Hanover in order to circumvent British laws forbidding the employment of foreigners. Reliable and protestant yet fluent in several languages and relatively uncomplaining, they made a welcome change from the standard British diplomat or colonial governor. Notable among them were the Pictet family who represented the British government in Geneva for much of the eighteenth century (in a reversal of roles, a Pictet recently served as Swiss ambassador in London), Frederic Haldimand of Lausanne, an early British governor of Montreal, and François Louis de Pesme, Sieur de St. Saphorin, who represented George I in Vienna for almost the whole of his reign.

It is St. Saphorin's friend, Lucas Schaub of Basle (1690-1758), who was perhaps the most successful and influential. When still in his twenties he became the secretary and right-hand man of the leading secretary of state, James Stanhope. In that capacity he drafted this letter from George I to the German Emperor announcing that he, Schaub, would be going on to Vienna from Paris with interesting proposals for an alliance between George, the Emperor, the French Regent and the Dutch. While the alliance was largely Stanhope's creation, some of its provisions had a distinctly Swiss tinge, which were almost certainly attributable to Schaub – such as the suggestion that a neutral Swiss peace-keeping force should garrison some of the crisis points in Italy. Schaub soon won George I's trust and later that of George II and his Queen. After Stanhope's death, he served in Paris for three years and, in the 1740s, in Germany and Poland.

After 1800 it finally became impossible for aliens to serve in the British diplomatic service under any pretexts, but certain modern British diplomatic dynasties, notably the Mallets, originated in Switzerland.

Draft of letter of George I to Emperor Charles VI, January 1718 in hand of Schaub.

Add. MS 61547, f. 83.

Portrait of
Sir Lucas Schaub of Basle,
when George I's envoy
to France, by
Hyacinthe Rigaud, 1722.
Reproduced by permission
of the Oeffentliche
Kunstsammlung
Basel Kunstmuseum.

II.6.7 *A Romantic Attachment*

The young Edward Gibbon (1737-1794), the author of *The Decline and Fall of the Roman Empire*, spent five years from 1753 in Lausanne. There he met and fell in love with Suzanne Curchod. As he later wrote, he found her 'learned without pedantry, lively in conversation, pure in sentiment and elegant in manners'. After his return to England, however, his father refused him permission to marry and 'after a painful struggle I yielded to my fate; I sighed as a lover, I obeyed as a son'.

II.6.6

The British Library possesses Suzanne's anguished letters on learning of his decision, but this letter dating from the height of their romance helps to explain why Suzanne so entranced the twenty year-old Gibbon. Writing from the loneliness of a snow-bound Crassy, 'Zimerline' gently teases him for neglecting her during her recent illness, and skittishly states that she has concluded that she must have 'quelques grains de coquetterie' in her character, 'for that is what ill-intentioned people – you for example – call a mild desire to please'.

Suzanne eventually became the wife of Jacques Necker, the Genevan banker and reformer of the finances of France, and mother of the celebrated society hostess and writer Madame de Staël. In time she was reconciled with Gibbon, who never forgot Switzerland. The British Library possesses the manuscript of the unfinished history of Switzerland which he began, in French, in the 1760s. In his will he bequeathed the best books in his library to the public library of the Academy of Lausanne, and one hundred guineas to its poor.

Letter from Suzanne Curchod to Edward Gibbon, 10 January 1758.   *Add. MS 34886, f.25.*

II.6.8 *A Very English Swiss*

Samuel Hieronymus Grimm of Burgdorf near Berne (1733-1794) was one of several Swiss artists to work in England in the eighteenth century. If Henry Fuseli (Johann Heinrich Füssli) of Zurich and Angelica Kauffmann of Chur are better known, Grimm merits a special place not only because of his considerable skill but because of the very Englishness of his work. Yet Grimm first came to England only when he was thirty five and his teacher, Johann Ludwig Aberli (1723-1786) of Berne, the foremost and most influential Swiss landscape artist of his time, was one of the earliest recorders of the grandeur of the Alps: far removed from the charm and frequent humour of Grimm's English work.

The British Library possesses many hundreds of pencil and ink and wash drawings and numerous watercolours commissioned from Grimm by the clergyman, Sir Richard Kaye (1736-1809), and by the Sussex antiquary Sir William Burrell (1732-1796). This lively watercolour of Lewes in Sussex, shows Grimm at his best. Looking from the heights to the east up Cliffe High Street, School Hill and the High Street towards the castle and surrounding Downs, one sees the town on a sunny summer's day some two hundred years ago. Accuracy is blended with an awareness of the picturesque and there is not a hint of the lifelessness so often found in topographical views.

Another of Grimm's clients, Gilbert White, whose famous book, *The Natural History of Selborne* he illustrated, described in a letter how Grimm 'first of all sketches his scapes with a lead-pencil; then he pens them all over, as he calls it, with Indian ink, rubbing out the superfluous pencil-strokes; then he gives a charming shading with a brush dipped in Indian ink; and last he throws a light tinge of watercolours over the whole'.

Samuel Hieronymus Grimm, *'A Bird's-Eye View of Lewes Town & the Cliffe with the adjacent Country taken from Baldy's Garden in the Cliffe'*, 1785. Pen, ink and watercolour. 250 x 390 mm.

Add. MS 5672, f.7 no. 11

II.6.9   *With Captain Cook in Tahiti*

John Webber (1751-1793) was the son of Abraham Wäber, a sculptor from Berne who came to England and anglicised his name in the early 1740s. At the age of five he was sent to Berne to be brought up by an aunt. There he, like his friend Grimm, was trained by Aberli before continuing his education in Paris. He was not to return to England until 1775. Little more than a year later his work caught the attention of Captain Cook's associate, Daniel Carl Solander, and in July 1776 he left England as draughtsman on what was to be Captain Cook's third and last voyage of exploration.

Although Cook prosaically wrote that 'Mr. Webber was engaged . . . for the express purpose of supplying the unavoidable imperfections of written accounts', of depicting 'everything that was curious, both within and without doors', many of his drawings and watercolours are far more than simple records. Webber states at the bottom right edge of this watercolour that this idyllic scene was 'drawn from nature'. Its composition, with the mountains descending to the water at the centre, nevertheless strongly resembles that of several watercolours of Alpine scenes by Aberli. After his return to England following Cook's murder, which he witnessed, Webber used his drawings as the basis for later watercolours and oil paintings and engraved several of them for publication. Other English watercolourists born of Swiss fathers at this time were John Alexander Gresse (1741-1794) and Jacob Schnebbelie (1760-1792).

John Webber, View in Vaitepiha Valley [August 1777]. Inscribed *'view of Hothiheite Peha drawn from nature by John Webber del ['del'* crossed out and replaced by *'n'] 77'*. Pen, wash and watercolour. 447 x 635 mm.   *Add MS 15513, f.13.*

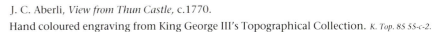
J. C. Aberli, *View from Thun Castle*, c.1770.
Hand coloured engraving from King George III's Topographical Collection. *K. Top. 85 55-c-2.*

II.6.9

11.6.10 *Turner at Chillon*

The short-lived peace of Amiens enabled Turner to visit Switzerland in 1802. He found the scenery of the country 'on the whole surpasses Wales and Scotland too'. He made numerous sketches on this trip and these he worked up into oil paintings or highly finished watercolours, often (as here) years later. He made a drawing of the Lake of Brienz which is dated 1809 for Sir John Swinburne and since the present sheet was also made for him it seems reasonable to date it about the same year. A similar but more extensive view in oils entitled 'Lake Geneva above Vevey' with Chillon in the distance was exhibited at the Royal Academy in 1810. Turner's watercolours of Swiss scenes were to reach their apogee between 1840-1846.

The Castle of Chillon, c.1809. Watercolour with some scraping out; 280 x 395 mm. Inscribed lower left: *'JMW Turner RA'*
Bequeathed by R.W. Lloyd. *1958-7-12-410.*
Reproduced by permission of the Trustees of the British Museum.

11.6.11 *The Prisoner of Chillon*

Lord Byron's poem, *The Prisoner of Chillon*, is the most celebrated of all English literary works to be inspired by Switzerland and its history. It was written following Byron's visit to the Castle of Chillon on the shores of the Lake of Geneva, and is derived from the heroic story of François de Bonnivard (1496-1570), a Genevan patriot imprisoned there by the Duke of Savoy from 1530 to 1536. This is a fair copy of the poem in the hand of Shelley's future wife, Mary Godwin, with extensive emendations by Byron, written in a notebook with marbled orange, black and blue paper covers. The manuscript is what Byron called the 'first copy' from his draft. The draft is at Yale, and the second copy in the possession of the publisher John Murray. It is dated at the beginning 'June 30th 1816' and signed and dated at the end 'Byron July 2d 1816'. It is inscribed 'Scrope Davies' inside the back cover.

The very existence of this manuscript was totally unsuspected until 1976 when it was discovered in a small trunk which had been deposited 150 years before in what is now Barclays Bank, Pall Mall East in London. The depositor was the dandy and gambler Scrope Berdmore Davies, who had been an intimate friend of Lord Byron, and who had recently lost all that he possessed, and a great deal more besides, at the tables. Into the little trunk he stuffed an astonishing

11.6.11: opening containing the description of the Castle.
Note the important changes to the wording made by Byron.

mixture of letters, bank statements, receipted bills, tennis club accounts and three literary treasures of the first order: two poetical notebooks of Byron and one of Shelley. The story of how these treasures found their way into the trunk begins with a holiday in Switzerland 175 years ago.

After leaving England for the last time on 25 April 1816 Byron settled for the summer at Cologny, a suburb of Geneva, overlooking the lake. Towards the end of May he met for the first time his fellow poet Shelley at the Hotel d'Angleterre at Secheron, the village next to Cologny. They were brought together by Claire Clairmont who had succeeded in making herself Byron's mistress shortly before his departure from England. She was the step-sister of Mary Godwin who in turn was the mistress, and later the wife, of Shelley. During the first weeks of June the Shelley party installed themselves in the Maison Chappuis, near the shores of the lake, while Byron took the Villa Diodati, a few hundred yards inland but raised on a hill. There followed a summer fruitful for English poetry. Byron and Shelley were impressed by each other and met almost every day. They shared a love of sailing, and a voyage around the lake together gave the world Byron's *The Prisoner of Chillon*, more stanzas for the Third Canto of his *Childe Harold*, and Shelley's 'Hymn to intellectual Beauty'.

On 29 July 1816 Byron's two closest friends, John Cam Hobhouse and Scrope Berdmore Davies, set out to join him in Switzerland. They went to Schaffhausen, inspected the Rhine Falls, visited Zurich which they found crammed with English, passed through Lucerne and came to Berne where they 'hailed the capital of the wisest Government in Europe'. At last, on 26 August, they joined Byron at Diodati.

Three days later Shelley and his party set out to return to England. With him he took a notebook containing Claire's transcripts of Canto III of *Childe Harold* and the *Prisoner of Chillon*, together with several other short poems written by Byron during that summer, to be delivered to Byron's publisher John Murray. With him Byron kept his draft of Canto III of *Childe Harold*, a fair copy in his own hand, and another transcript in Mary Godwin's hand. Until the discovery of Scrope Davies's trunk this was all we knew, though it was presumed possible that Byron had kept with him the drafts of *The Prisoner of Chillon* and at least some other poems.

On 2 September Byron gave Scrope Davies the fair copy in his own hand of Canto III, not only as a present, but also so that he could show it to John Murray for comparison with Claire's transcript 'in such parts as it may chance to be difficult to decipher'. Although there is no mention of it either in letters or elsewhere, we must presume that at the same time, or nearly so, Byron gave Scrope Davies the present manuscript as well.

On 5 September Scrope Davies left Geneva for London. His kindness in undertaking the various errands with which Byron had entrusted him was for

11.6.11: the closing page with Byron's signature.

long ill-rewarded. All that was known of the business was a series of letters from Byron to his publisher Murray enquiring ever more anxiously whether he had received the *Childe Harold* manuscript. In the final letter, written from Venice on 4 December, Byron said:

> There are some things I wanted and want to know - viz whether Mr. Davies of inaccurate memory had or had not delivered the M.S. as delivered to him – because if he has not – you will find that he will bountifully bestow extracts and transcriptions to all the curious of his acquaintance – in which case you may possibly find your publication anticipated by the 'Cambridge' or other Chronicles.

This letter, together with the fact that the whereabouts of the manuscript remained unknown, led students of Byron to conclude that Scrope, so far from faithfully delivering the manuscript to Murray, had never been near him and had kept it for himself. The fact was, however, that Byron had not been kept up to date with events. Scrope had not only taken the manuscripts to Murray, but had remained in constant touch with him while they defended Byron's interests against one James Johnston, bookseller of Cheapside and Oxford Street, seeking to restrain Johnston from publishing certain poems which he had advertised as being by Byron, but which were in fact completely spurious. On 25 November Scrope had sworn an affidavit, saying:

> That he . . . on or about the latter end of August or the beginning of September last parted from the said Complainant [Byron] near Geneva and brought from the said Complainant to John Murray . two of the last new Poems written by the said Complainant being the Third Canto of Childe Harold and the Prisoner of Chillon.

Scrope did, therefore, faithfully discharge his commission from Byron, and take both manuscripts to Murray. By the time he arrived, however, the poems were set up in print and Murray, having no use for them, returned the manuscripts to Scrope. In this way were three major literary treasures lost from sight for 156 years – but were preserved in perfect condition for our generation to enjoy.

George Gordon, Lord Byron, *The Prisoner of Chillon*. MS 'first copy' with corrections, 30 June-2 July 1816. Octavo; ff. 14.   *Scrope Davis MS 7*

Receipt by François de Bonnivard, 'The Prisoner of Chillon' of Byron's poem, to the Syndics and Council of Geneva; Berne, 16 March 1541.
Add. MS 39672, f.16.

11.6.12 *The Swiss Abroad*

Because of the long history of emigration forced by poverty, there can hardly be a village in Switzerland that does not have houses built by returned emigrés or examples of emigré generosity or piety. Such is their importance that the Swiss abroad are formally recognised as the 'Fifth Switzerland' after the German, French, Italian and Romansch-speaking Switzerlands.

The Unione Ticinese is one of the oldest surviving Swiss societies in England. It was founded in 1874 as a benevolent society for working class Ticinesi, predominantly waiters and chefs from the Val di Blenio in the north of the canton. They had been coming in ever-increasing numbers to work in the numerous London restaurants and other enterprises run by the Gatti family from Dongio (Val di Blenio) since the 1850s, when an Austrian blockade sealed off Lombardy, their principal traditional area of seasonal emigration. Gatti's establishments, which began as chestnut and coffee stalls, became the first modern restaurants, as opposed to taverns and chop houses, in Britain and by 1900 most of the 'Italian' restaurants in England were owned by Ticinesi. Music halls were staged in Gatti establishments on or near the Strand, and the Gattis and their circle also manufactured chocolate, owned West End theatres, founded the electricity company that served most of central London before 1947 and created what became the largest ice importing concern in the Britain.

This invitation to the Society's fiftieth anniversary celebrations at Monico's, one of the Italian Swiss restaurants in Central London, shows two girls in Ticinese dress standing in front of the Castel Grande in Bellinzona, the cantonal capital, and looking towards St. Paul's Cathedral and Tower Bridge. It was designed by the Swiss artist Paul Tanner (1882-1934). Giuseppe Motta, whose words are quoted below, was a Ticinese who served for many years as Switzerland's foreign minister, and periodically, president.

The last of the restaurants deriving from the Gattis passed out of Ticinese hands a few years ago, but the Unione Ticinese continues to thrive with a membership drawn from descendants of the original waiters and chefs and from newer arrivals. Most have dual nationality and maintain close links with the Ticino while playing a full part in British life and a distinctive role in that of the Swiss community in Britain.

Commemorative invitation to 50th anniversary dinner of the Unione Ticinese at Monico's, 14 February 1924.

Loaned by Frank Allegranza

III *SWISS QUALITY*

III.1. *Swiss Printmakers*

This small group of prints by artists who were either born in Switzerland, were Swiss in origin or who became Swiss citizens has been chosen to suggest, albeit inadequately and incompletely, the rich and varied contribution to graphic art made by the inhabitants of the 'Land of Mountains'. There are two points to note concerning the selection. First, only works originally created as prints have been included and for this reason reproductive prints have been deliberately avoided. Secondly, there has been no attempt to produce anything resembling an historical or artistic 'survey' of Swiss printmaking. Instead the aim has been to show through the variety of media employed, a wide date span and by a choice of very different artists, prints which are of undoubted interest and some significance not merely in the context of Switzerland but also in the larger one of the history of printmaking as a whole.

III.1.1. *Nikolaus Manuel Deutsch (1484-1530)*

Three of the *Wise Virgins* from a series of eight entitled *The Wise and Foolish Virgins*. 1518.

Woodcuts; each 185 x 108 mm.

Deutsch was born in Berne where he also died. He was a painter, poet and politician who served as a member of Berne City Council from 1510 until his death. Much influenced by Dürer, Baldung, Urs Graf and Lucas Cranach the Elder, Deutsch's work is well represented in the museums in Berne and Basle. His celebrated wall-painting, *The Dance of Death* (c.1516-19) made for the Dominicans in Berne was destroyed in 1660 and is now known only from copies.

1877-6-9-63, 64, 60.

III.1.2. *Urs Graf (c.1485-1529/30)*

Pyramus and Thisbe

Woodcut; 314 x 222 mm.

Graf was a goldsmith and designer of glass-paintings, woodcuts and etchings. He was born in Solothurn where he trained with his father who was also a goldsmith and by 1507 he was working both in Basle and in Zurich. Throughout his career he was much in demand as a book-illustrator and he was prolific in his supply of designs to printers in Strasbourg, Paris and Basle. This independent single sheet print which does not seem to have been made as an illustration was designed by Graf but the block was cut by a little-known woodcutter named Krüger.

The legend of Pyramus and Thisbe tells of the passion of a young man of Babylon for the lovely maiden Thisbe. Arranging to meet one night against their parents' wishes, Thisbe arrived first and, seeing a lion, fled into the woods, leaving her cloak behind. When Pyramus came to the scene he found the cloak torn by the lion and, imagining his lover dead, killed himself with his sword. Thisbe on her return found the dead Pyramus and in her anguish ended her own sufferings on the same sword.

1837-6-16-248

III.1.3. *Hans Holbein the Younger (1497/8-1543)*

The Dance of Death. Before 1526

Eight woodcuts by Hans Lützelburger (d. 1526); each 65 x 50 mm.

The subjects are as follows: *The Countess, The Noblewoman, The Duchess, The Shop-Keeper, The Ploughman, The Child, The Last Judgement* and *The Coat of Arms of Death.*

41 of these celebrated illustrations (there were 58 in all) were first published in Lyon in 1538. They were subsequently increased in number and frequently reprinted proving enormously influential. Holbein made his preparatory drawings c. 1524-5.

Holbein was born in Augsburg but completed several important commissions chiefly in Basle but also in Lucerne. In 1519 he was admitted to the painters' guild in Basle and became a citizen in the following year.

Lützelburger was the most distinguished cutter who worked for Holbein and was one of the few Renaissance woodcutters to have achieved wide fame in his own right.

Presented by W. Mitchell 1895-1-22-826, 827, 825, 819, 821, 831, 833, 834.

III.1.4 *Jost Amman (1539-1591)*

A Bear Hunt

Water-fowl shooting

A Fishing Party

Falconing scene and Partridge Hunt with nets

Four etchings from a set of eight; each 41 x 46 mm.

Amman was born in Zurich but worked in Basle, Nuremberg, Augsburg, Frankfurt, Heidelberg and Würzburg. Extremely prolific, he produced quantities of ornamental and heraldic prints, title-pages and miscellaneous book-illustrations. He was at his best in his portrait prints and in unpretentious scenes of everyday life of which these hunts are good examples. Prints such as these were intended mainly as models to be used by craftsmen in the decorative arts and were rarely considered to be more than means or suggestions to further ends.

1874-7-11-1309   1922-4-10-212   1874-7-11-1308   1870-5-14-380

III.1.5. *Jean Étienne Liotard (1702-1789)*

Self Portrait 1781

Engraving, etching, roulette and rocker; 480 x 397 mm.

Proof before letters. The lettered state is dated 1781 and bears a text reading 'Effet clair obscur sans sacrifice'.

Liotard was born in Geneva although his family was of French origin. In 1723 he moved to Paris to begin a dazzling career primarily as a pastellist and portraitist. He travelled widely, becoming particularly celebrated during his 15 year stay in Istanbul (Constantinople) where he made numerous portraits of members of the ruling families.

His prints, although few in number, are of great interest not only artistically but also from a technical point of view – this self portrait being a sophisticated *melange* of effects. After an adventurous and full life he returned to Geneva where he died.

1931-4-13-518

III.1.6 *Henry Fuseli (Johann Heinrich Füssli) (1741-1825)*

Mrs Fuseli on a divan looking out of a window 1802

Pen lithograph; 315 x 200 mm.

Inscribed in reversed letters on the stone in Greek 'Evening thou bringest all'.

Made after Fuseli's own painting in the Goethe Museum, Frankfurt, this print was included in part 4 of *Specimens of Polyautography* (c.1806-7) which was the earliest publication of artists' lithographs in England. As a composition it must rank as one of the most unashamedly sensual prints ever made.

Fuseli was born in Zurich, of a family of artists (see II.1.11), and came to England in 1764 where he was given much encouragement by Reynolds. In 1769 he went to Rome and remained in Italy for eight years. In 1789 he returned to England and the following year was appointed Professor of Painting at the Royal Academy, a position he was to hold almost until his death.

1867-12-14-419

III.1.7 *Angelica Kauffmann (1741-1807)*

A seated Woman 1766

Head of a Woman 1770

Etchings; 212 x 165 mm. and 128 x 97 mm.

Kauffmann was born in Chur where her father, a painter himself, fostered her prodigious and precocious talents both as painter and musician. Early in her career she was faced with the dilemma of whether to become an artist or an operatic singer. Opting for the former she moved to England where she spent most of her working life, becoming a founder member of the Royal Academy in 1768.

Today she is perhaps best known for the numerous allegorical and mythological paintings which she made for Adam interiors and which were made very popular during her own lifetime by being much reproduced in the form of stipple engravings. These etchings show that she was also an accomplished printmaker - an aspect of her work which is perhaps less familiar.

1847-7-23-86

1868-12-12-147

III.1.9. *Felix Vallotton (1865-1925)*

Le Bain 1894

Woodcut; 181 x 225 mm.

Vallotton was born in Lausanne but moved to Paris at the age of seventeen and became a French citizen in 1900.

By February 1892 he was being hailed as one of the leaders in an important area of the Paris artistic avant-garde: the revival of the original woodcut.

Vallotton was strongly influenced by Japanese woodcuts but unlike other artists similarly affected he was never tempted to add colour to his woodcuts. Instead he exploited to the full the great potential for abstraction offered by the medium with its flat black and white contrast. Octave Uzanne, a contemporary critic and woodcut enthusiast, wrote excitedly that Vallotton 'has cut into blocks of tender pear wood diverse scenes of contemporary life with the artlessness of a woodcutter of the sixteenth century'.

III.1.8. *Théophile-Alexandre Steinlen (1859-1923)*

La Rue Caulaincourt 1896

Lithograph; 252 x 358 mm.

Steinlen was born in Lausanne where his father was a post office official. He studied at the University of Lausanne but in 1881 moved to Montmartre in Paris where he was to remain for the rest of his life.

He rejected traditional salon painting as well as Impressionism and Post-Impressionism. Instead he went his own way, concentrating on book and journal illustration, seeing himself essentially as an artist of the people and remaining to the end an ardent socialist and realist.

He used lithography with particular skill and it was this medium which seemed to suit his subject matter better than almost any other.

1897-2-10-71

Bequeathed by Campbell Dodgson 1949-4-11-4598

III.1.10 Paul Klee (1879-1940)

Woman and Beast 1904

Etching on zinc; 200 x 228 mm.

Klee was born in Münchenbuchsee near Berne to a Swiss mother and a German father and spent his early years in Switzerland. In 1898 he moved to Munich to study art and in 1901 made his first etching. In October 1904 he visited the Munich Museum Print Room where he admired the work of Goya, Blake and Aubrey Beardsley. Clearly influenced by what he had seen he made this print in the following month, including it in a series which he called *Inventions*, in which he explored grotesque distortions of the human body. He worked in Germany for many years and in 1920 became a *Formmeister* of the newly established *Bauhaus* in Weimar. In 1933 the Nazis dismissed him from the Düsseldorf Academy in their effort to excise modernism from German cultural institutions and as a result Klee sought and obtained Swiss citizenship.

He died in Muralto (Locarno) in 1940.

Presented by the Contemporary Art Society 1945-12-8-214

III.1.11 Kurt Seligmann (1900-1962)

Abstract composition 'Le Eilibustier' 1934

Etching; 352 x 288 mm.

From a set entitled *Protuberances Cardiaques*

Born in Basle, Seligmann exhibited from 1918 to 1932 chiefly in his birthplace and in Berne. He moved to Paris and in 1934 produced a set of fifteen etchings including the present sheet in which he explored symbolism combining both figurative and abstract elements. He became a member of the Surrealist movement and in 1939 settled in the United States. Continuing his interest in Surrealism by writing as well as painting and printmaking, he became increasingly preoccupied

with the occult. He died as the result of an accident at Sugar Loaf in New York State in 1962.

1980-3-22-21

III.1.12 Serge Brignoni (1903 -)

Anatomie 1 or *Métamorphose*

Relief etching with engraving, softground etching and aquatint on tin; 150 x 241 mm.

Brignoni was born in Chiasso, not far from the Molas' birthplace of Coldrerio (see II.5.5; II.3.49), and studied first in Berne, moving to Berlin in 1922. There he became interested in the work of artists of the School of Paris and on settling there, became a student of André Lhote, an artist with whom he was soon to collaborate. He worked in the influential Atelier 17 studio throughout the 1930s with its founder Stanley William Hayter, returning to Switzerland in 1940.

He became associated with the Surrealist movement and in this vein has produced paintings and sculptures as well as prints. He has had exhibitions throughout the world and his works can be found in most major Swiss public collections.

1989-3-14-18

III.2 *Watchmaking in Switzerland*

Swiss watchmaking dates back to the 16th century; the first centres were Zug and Geneva.

Little is known about Zug: the watches made there are broadly of the German type, and the tradition appears to have died out during the second half of the 17th century.

Genevan watchmaking was much more successful; this was essentially a French-based tradition, from which the entire subsequent Swiss watch industry developed. From the very beginning Geneva produced work of high quality, but from about 1680 there was also an increasing trade in cheap, mass-produced watches (often signed with fictitious names), which were exported throughout Europe and beyond. In the course of the 18th century this trade spread to the territory around La Chaux-de-Fonds, which gradually took over from Geneva. During the 19th century the quality was much improved, but even so the introduction of high-quality machine-produced watches from America was a severe blow to the Swiss in the 1870s. As a result they, too, began to use machines extensively, and recovered much of the market. The second and more severe blow came in the 1950s, with the introduction of cheap Japanese quartz watches, and the trade has since languished.

Throughout the 19th and 20th centuries Geneva itself remained a centre for high quality watches, and it is still the home of such famous firms as Vacheron & Constantin, Audemars Piguet, Patek Philippe and Rolex.

Over the centuries several important watchmakers emigrated from Switzerland. The most important ones were: Jost Bürgi (1552-1632) of Kassel and Prague (see II.5.3); Ferdinand Berthoud (1727-1807) and Abraham Louis Breguet, (1747-1823) of Paris. The important London watchmakers Justin Vulliamy (1730-ca. 1790) and Josiah Emery (ca. 1725-1797) were also of Swiss origin.

Clocks and Watches by Swiss Makers, or Makers who had Emigrated from Switzerland, on Permanent Display in the British Museum

A. *Watches (all in Area 7).*
Section 2: The Stackfreed
*Nr. 4: Hans Jacob Zurlauben, Zug, *circa* 1650 .

A.4.

Section 3: The Balance spring
Nr. 3: Malacrida, Berne, *circa* 1680-5.
Nr. 9: Jos. Emery, London, *circa* 1784.
Nr. 11: Anon, *circa* 1875.

Section 5: Repeating Mechanisms,
Nr. 8: Abraham Louis Breguet, Paris, 1810.
Nr. 11: Anon, *circa* 1876-8.

Section 6: Cylinder Escapement
Nr. 4: Abraham Louis Breguet, Paris, 1798.
Nr. 12: Anon, *circa* 1876-8.

Section 7: Duplex Escapement
Nr. 4: Vauchez Frères, Fleurier, *circa* 1840.
Nr. 6: Jos. Emery, London, *circa* 1790.
Nr. 8: Anon, *circa* 1825.
Nr. 11: Anon, (Fleurier), *circa* 1860.

Section 8: Keyless Winding
Nr. 2: Abraham Louis Breguet, Paris, 1791.
Nr. 10: Anon, *circa* 1915.
Nr. 12: Anon, *circa* 1920

Section 9: Lever Escapement I
*Nr. 2: Jos. Emery, London, 1786.

Section 10: Lever Escapement II
Nr. 3: Breguet et Fils, Paris *circa* 1810.
Nr. 5: Anon, 1850.
Nr. 7: Georges-Frederic Roskopf,
   La Chaux-de-Fonds, *circa* 1870.

Section 12: Temperature Compensation
Nr. 1: Ferd. Berthoud, Paris, 1763.
Nr. 6: Paul Dittisheim,
   La Chaux-de-Fonds, 1915.
Nr. 11: Ferd. Berthoud, Paris, *circa* 1760.

B. *Enamel cases.*
*Nr. 8: Les frères Huaut les jeunes and
   Jacques Descombes, Geneva, *circa* 1685.
Nr. 10: Aguiton & Rochat, Geneva.
*Nr. 14: Bovet, Fleurier, *circa* 1830.

C. *Gold cases.*
Nr. 16: Abraham Louis Breguet, Paris.
Nr. 17: Abraham Louis Breguet, Paris.
Nr. 18: Anon, *circa* 1920.

D. *Silver cases.*
Nr. 17: Demelais, Geneva, *circa* 1750.

E. *Various cases.*
Nr. 2: Jacques Sermand, Geneva, *circa* 1630.
Nr. 4: M. Kappelin, Lucerne, *circa* 1650.
Nr. 8: Wilhelm Peffenhauser, Zug, *circa* 1650.
Nr. 9: Charles Bobinet, Geneva, *circa* 1650.
Nr. 18: Neuron & Co., Geneva, *circa* 1800.
Nr. 19: Anon, (Geneva?), *circa* 1820.

F. *Chronometers and clocks.*
Area 12
Abraham Louis Breguet, Paris.
(several objects).

Enamelled watch made for export to China by Bovet of Fleurier near Neuchatel, *circa* 1830.

B.14.

B.8.

Enamelled case by Jean-Pierre and Ami Huaut with movement by Jacques Descombes, Geneva, *cira* 1685.

9.2.

Watch by Josiah Emery of Geneva, working in Charing Cross, 1786

III.3 *The Coins and Medals of Switzerland*

J. Dassier: Geneva, 1749

[III.3.108]

Switzerland's position in the centre of Europe has ensured that it has played an active role in the history of European coinage. Swiss imitations of the gold staters of Philip II of Macedon were in all probability the principal source for the tradition of gold coinage of Celtic Gaul, and so ultimately Celtic Britain. The Romans imported coins into the province of Raetia, but from the 6th century until the 16th successive Frankish, Carolingian and imperial lords established important mints in several Swiss towns. In the 13th and 14th centuries the mints of the cities, bishops, abbots and local rulers of Switzerland fully participated in the German practice of issuing the almost paper-thin coins known as bracteates. In the late 15th century Swiss portrait coins rivalled their Italian prototypes. In modern times the country's strategic importance within Europe led to the Napoleonic invasion and the coinage of the Helvetic Republic. In 1865 Switzerland once again took centre stage in the monetary history of Europe, with its participation in the Latin Monetary Union.

The tension between the need for unity, dictated by the country's position as a small state surrounded by larger and more powerful neighbours, and the cultural, religious and linguistic diversity of her people has had an important effect on the history of Swiss coinage. From medieval times on, a wide range of images, emblems and portraits was characteristic of the coinage, as was a variety of local monetary systems. Attempts at standardisation of weights and denominations were made at a series of conventions held from the 15th century on, but a permanent solution was invariably thwarted by cantonal rivalry. Only in the mid 19th century was a national currency adopted. Since

then the designs of the coins have scarcely altered. This reflects the stability of the Swiss nation over the past one and a half centuries, but may also be indicative of Swiss caution, an alleged national attribute which has in the past also been used to explain the large size of some banknotes: the size inspires confidence!

Switzerland has provided Europe with a handful of medallists of international repute, and has also seen a number of flourishing local schools. Jakob Stampfer, who worked in Zurich in the 16th century, produced cast and chased medals, one of which, showing the oath of Eternal Federation, attained huge popularity and has been widely imitated up to the present century. Gaspare Mola, one of the leading medallists and coin engravers of Baroque Italy, was a native of the Mendrisiotto, one of the Swiss-ruled bailiwicks south of the Gotthard, who like so many of his countrymen had to pursue his career outside the Confederation. Jean and Jacques Antoine Dassier of Geneva were amongst the most celebrated medallists of the 18th century. Both also worked in England, where Jean was offered a position at the Royal Mint which he declined. Jacques Antoine was active in Italy and was later employed as an engraver at the mints of London and St. Petersburg. Amongst other Swiss medallists one might mention a group originating from Neuchatel: the Thiébaud family, Jean-Pierre Droz and Henri-François Brandt. But to pick out individuals is an invidious task, for the 18th and 19th centuries witnessed a proliferation of Swiss medallic activity, which the need for both prize and shooting medals at the numerous federal and cantonal shooting festivals was to fuel. Suffice to say that, of 19th century medallists, Antoine and Hugues Bovy and Hans Frei were amongst the most distinguished. Frei worked on into the present century, but the Swiss medal did not die with him. A glance through the catalogues of the international medallic exhibitions of the post-War period shows that Switzerland still produces medallists of talent.

Swiss Coinage Before Switzerland

The earliest coins to be struck in what is now Switzerland were Celtic issues of the 3rd century B.C. The designs imitate the gold staters of the Macedonian King Philip II; later silver coins followed Roman Republican types. As the Roman province of Raetia, no coins were issued, and it was only in the 6th century A.D., after much of present day Switzerland had been incorporated into the kingdom of the Franks, that mints were established. As part of the Carolingian empire, Switzerland possessed a reduced number of mints. Imperial mints continued to operate in Switzerland long after the establishment of the Swiss Confederation, for example, in Basle which was still working in the 16th century.

The Celts

III.3.1 Quarter stater of Unterendfelden (Zurich) type. 2nd century B.C. AV. 1919-2-13-995. Presented by Sir Arthur Evans.

III.3.2 Stater of the Helvetii. 1st century B.C. AV. 1848-1-24-1.

III.3.3 Coin of the Sequani. About 100 B.C. AR. 1901-5-3-575.

The Franks

*III.3.4 Lausanne. Tremissis. About 580 A.D. AV. R 11256.

III.3.5 Avenches. Tremissis. 7th century. AV. R 11257.

III.3.6 Geneva. Tremissis. 7th century. AV. R 11236.

III.3.7 Sion (Sitten). Tremissis. 7th century. AV. 1855-2-16-8.

III.3.4

The Carolingians

III.3.8 Constance. Denier of Louis the Child (899-911). AR. 1838-7-10-1219.

The Holy Roman Empire

III.3.9 Basle. Denier of Conrad II (1024-39). AR. 1854-5-25-1.

III.3.10 Berne. Bracteate of Frederick II (1212-50). AR. 1856-4-10-41.

III.3.11 Basle. Gulden of Sigismund (1410-37). AV. Townshend, p. 21, 1. 1856-8-1-36.

III.3.12 Basle. Gulden of Maximilian. 1516. AV. 1857-9-10-32.

The Rise of Local Coinage

III.3.28

From the 10th century the Emperors used the granting of minting rights as a means of retaining support. The dukes of Swabia were amongst the first to be rewarded in this way. The establishment of

mints in various abbeys and bishoprics in the 10th and 11th centuries led to a predominance of ecclesiastical coinage. The increasing importance of the cities is reflected in the growing number permitted to strike coinage from the 13th century on. In the 13th and 14th centuries a number of local rulers were allowed to mint coins for short periods, including the Habsburgs.

Local rulers

III.3.13 Zurich. Denier of Hermann I, Duke of Swabia (926-48). AR. Townshend. p. 512, 1. C 4223.

III.3.14 Burgdorf. Bracteate of Hartmann III, Count of Kyburg (1353-77). AR. Townshend, p. 257,3.

III.3.15 Laufenburg. Bracteate of Rudolph IV, Count of Habsburg-Laufenburg. 1377. AR. 1853-6-28-13.

The Church

III.3.16 Lausanne. Denier of the bishopric, 11th-13th centuries. AR. C 4554. Armitage bequest. Townshend, p. 261, 13.

III.3.17 Geneva. Denier of Bishop Conrad (1019-31). AR. Townshend, p. 630, 1. 1856-4-10-55.

III.3.18 Basle. Semi-bracteate of Bishop Theodoric (1041-57). AR. 1860-5-1-76. Presented by Count J.F.W. de Salis.

III.3.19 Chur. Denier of Bishop Henry II of Arbon (1180-93). AR. Townshend, p. 103,1. 1860-5-1-190. Presented by Count J.F.W. de Salis.

III.3.20 Zurich. Bracteate of the abbey of Frauenmünster. 14th-15th centuries. Billon. Townshend, p.515, 28.

III.3.21 Lausanne. Sol of Bishop Guy de Prangins (1375-92). AR. Townshend, p. 269.1.

III.3.22 Sion. Dicken of Bishop Jodocus von Silinen (1482-96). AR. Townshend, p.360.3.

*III.3.23 Sion. Testoon of Bishop Matthaeus Schiner (1499-1522). AR. Townshend, p. 364, 24.

*III.3.24 Sion. Double Taler of Bishop Matthaeus Schiner. 1501. AR. 1853-6-28-24.

III.3.24

The Cities and the Cantons

III.3.25 Schaffhausen. Bracteate. Late 13th century. AR. 1848-2-12-390.

III.3.26 Solothurn. Bracteate. 13th-14th centuries. Billon. Townshend, p.391, 17.

III.3.27 Diesenhofen. Bracteate. 14th century. AR. 1853-4-12-3.

*III.3.28 St. Gallen. Bracteate. Late 14th century. AR. Townshend, p 156,7.

III.3.29 Solothurn. Fünfer. 15th century. Billon. Townshend, p. 393, 43.

III.3.30 Berne. Dicken. 1492. AR. 1860-5-1-102. Presented by Count J.F.W. de Salis.

III.3.31 Freiburg. Dicken. 15th century. AR. 1860-5-1-235. Presented by Count J.F.W. de Salis.

III.3.32 St. Gallen. Dicken. 1504/5. AR. Townshend, p. 160, 15. Townshend, p. 160, 17.

III.3.33 Basle. Gulden. 1521. AV. Townshend, p. 22, 8.

Jakob Stampfer

Stampfer (1505-79) is Switzerland's most important medallist before Dassier and one of the foremost figures of Swiss 16th-century art. He worked principally in his native town of Zurich, as a medallist, engraver of coin-dies and goldsmith. His medals display the influence of contemporary German work. Amongst his subjects were several prominent Swiss reformers.

III.3.36

*III.3.34 Foundation of the Swiss Confederation. Medal. AR. Townshend, p. 589,2.

*III.3.35 Zwingli. Medal. 1531. AR. M 2840.

*III.3.36 The confederate cantons and the christening of Claudia, daughter of Henri II of France. Medal. 1547. AR. Townshend, p. 592, 12. 1913-12-4-136. Lady Ramsay bequest.

*III.3.37 Zug. Taler. 1565. Townshend, p. 489, 5. 1859-11-15-45.

III.3.38: (Reverse)   *III.3.39: (Reverse)*

The Age of the Reformation

The Reformation divided Switzerland. Many of those cantons which adopted protestantism secularised the iconography of their coins. For example, Zurich, reformed by Zwingli in 1523-5, replaced the three decapitated saints on its talers with coats of arms. In contrast, the talers of Lucerne, the centre of Catholic Switzerland, retained the martyrdom of St. Leodigarius. Alliances, both within the Confederation and international, reflect the religious differences.

*III.3.38   Zurich. Taler. 1512. AR. Townshend, p. 524,71. Townshend, p. 524, 72.

*III.3.39   Zurich. Taler. 1526. AR. 1859-11-15-37. Townshend, p.524,73.

III.3.40   Uri, Schwyz and Unterwalden. Dicken. 1561. AR. Townshend. p.450,4.

III.3.41   Uri, Schwyz and Unterwalden. Taler. 1561. AR. Townshend, p. 450,3.

III.3.42   Lucerne. Taler. 1557. AR. Townshend, p.281, 21.

III.3.43   Sion. Ducat of Bishop Hildebrand von Riedmatten (1565-1604). AV. Townshend, p.369,46.

*III.3.44   Gruyère [Greierz]. Pattern of a sol of Count Michael of Gruyère. 1552. AV. Townshend. p.632.

III.3.45   Alliance between Zurich, Berne and Strasbourg. Medal. 1588. AR. Townshend, p.593,15.

III.3.46   Alliance between Graubünden and Venice. Medal, 1588. AV. 1850- 5-2-31.

III.3.47   Geneva. 3 sols. 1589. Billon. Townshend, p.195, 60. Townshend, p. 195, 61.

III.3.48   Geneva. (emergency money). 1590. AE. Townshend, p.225,321. Townshend, p. 225, 322.

A Swiss Abroad

Gaspare Mola of Coldrerio (c.1580-1640), like many Swiss artists, pursued his career outside Switzerland. He was active as a medallist and coin engraver at the mints of Milan, Florence, Mantua and finally Rome. The medallist and goldsmith Gaspare Morone (1603-69) was his nephew. Other Swiss medallists to work abroad were the Dassiers, Johann Carl Hedlinger (1691-1771), Jean-Pierre Droz (1746-1823) and Joseph Niederöst (1804-56), the last of whom also worked in Florence.

*III.3.49   Vincenzo Gonzaga, Duke of Mantua (1587-1612). Medal. AE. George III Mantuan Medals 47.

Diversity of Religion and Cantons

Besides cantonal issues, local rulers retained the right to mint coins and ecclesiastical mints continued in operation until the establishment of the Helvetic Republic. This wide range of issues resulted in great confusion in matters of exchange which a series of conventions attempted with only limited success to address. The range of emblems on Swiss coinage was extended in the 17th century with the introduction of the city view, a type favoured especially by the protestant towns. Religious diversity is documented by the medals of the League of the Catholic cantons, and by those of the Second Villmergen War of 1712. Some of the prominent figures of the Swiss Enlightenment were commemorated on medals.

Cantons

III.3.50   Valais. Dicken. 1628. AR. Townshend, p. 477, 1. Townshend, p.477, 2.

III.3.51   Chur. 10 Kreutzer. 1631/2. Billon. 1850-5-2-32. Townshend, p. 117,6.

*III.3.52   Schaffhausen. Dicken. 1631. AR. Townshend, p. 332, 21.

III.3.52

III.3.53   Berne. 10 Ducats. 1681. AV. 1858-10-1-1.

III.3.54   Berne. Medal. 1698. AR. Townshend, p. 85,1.

III.3.55   Zurich. Taler. 1736. AR. 1840-10-10-21.

III.3.56   Basle. Taler. 1785. AR. Townshend, p.29,57.

*III.3.57   League of the Catholic cantons and Valais. Medal. 1696. AR. Townshend, p. 478,1.

III.3.58   Second Villmergen War. Medal by H.J. Gessner. 1712. AR. Townshend, p.595,21.

*III.3.59   Second Villmergen War. Medal by J. de Beyer. 1712. AR. 1981-6- 23-67.

III.3.60   Fidelity of Lausanne to Berne. Medal by J. Hug. 1723. AR. Townshend, p. 86,7.

*III.3.61   Uri. Ducat. 1720. AV. Townshend, p. 441,2.

III.3.62   Unterwalden. Taler. 1732. AR. 1860-5-1-530. Presented by Count J.F.W. de Salis.

III.3.61

III.3.63   Appenzell. Ducat. 1737. AV. Townshend, p.7,1.

III.3.64   Renewal of the League of the Catholic cantons and Valais. Medal by B.A. Stedelin. 1780. AR. Townshend, p.478,2. 1852-11-27-20.

III.3.65   Solothurn. Duplone. 1787. AV. Townshend, p. 391,38.

III.3.66   Berne. Taler. 1789. AR. Townshend, p.56,15.

Local rulers

III.3.67   Haldenstein. Dicken of Thomas I, Baron of Schauenstein-Haldenstein. 1620. AR. Townshend, p. 249,4.

III.3.68   Neuchâtel. Twelfth of an écu of Henri II, Duke of Longueville (1595-1663). AR. SSB 126-150. Presented by Miss Sarah Banks.

III.3.69   Roveredo. Triple scudo of Teodoro Trivulzio, Count of Mesocco. 1676. AR. Townshend, p.625,1.

The Church

III.3.70   Chur. 7 Ducats of Bishop Johann Flug von Aspermont. 1613. AV. Townshend, p. 106,11.

III.3.71   St. Gallen. Taler of Abbot Bernhard Müller. 1622. AR. Townshend, p. 149,1.

III.3.72   Basle. 2 Ducats of Bishop Johann Konrad von Reinach. 1716. AV. Townshend, p. 17,7.

III.3.73   Basle. 6 Batzen of Bishop Joseph von Roggenbach. 1788. Billon. 1860-5-1-97. Presented by Count J.F.W. de Salis. Townshend, p. 19, 26.

The Swiss Enlightenment

III.3.74   To distinguished scholars of Zurich. Medal by J.C. Mörikofer. AR. Townshend, p. 569,13.

III.3.75   Albrecht von Haller. Medal by J.M. Mörikofer. 1754 (?). AE. 1906-11-3-1654. Presented by Dr. F. Parkes Weber.

III.3.76   Johann Kaspar Lavater. Medal by H.H. Boltschauer. AR. 1863-11- 14-52. Presented by Count J.F.W. de Salis.

III.3.77   Jean Jacques Rousseau. Medal by T. Bonneton. 1793. AE gilt. Townshend, p. 227,7.

The Reformation Commemorated

*III.3.78   Calvin. Medal. 1552. AE. M 0652.

III.3.79   Calvin. Medal by S. Dadler. 1641. AR. Townshend, p.225,2. George III Illustrious Persons 279.

III.3.80   300th anniversary of the death of Calvin. Medal by H Bovy. 1864. AE. 1906-11-3-1628. Presented by Dr. F. Parkes Weber. 1978-12-19-35. Presented by Prof. and Mrs. J. Hull-Grundy.

III.3.81 200th anniversary of the Reformation at Geneva. Medal by J. Dassier. 1735. AE. M 1984.

*III.3.82 300th anniversary of the Reformation at Geneva. Medal by A. Bovy. 1835. AR, AE. Townshend, p.228,9. M1985. Presented by Mr. L. A. Lawrence.

III.3.82

III.3.83 300th anniversary of Beza's Geneva Academy. Medal by A. Bovet. 1859. AE. 1911-3-14-1. Presented by Mr. A.H.S. Yeames.

III.3.84 Zwingli. Medal by H.J. Gessner. 1719. AR. M 0461. Rev. C.M. Cracherode bequest.

III.3.85 Bullinger. Medal by H.J. Gessner. 1719. AE. M 0322.

III.3.86 300th anniversary of the Reformation at Winterthur. Medal by J. Aberli. 1819. AR. Townshend, p.480,1.

III.3.87 Haller and the 300th anniversary of the Reformation at Berne. Medal. 1828. AR. Townshend, p.85,4.

III.3.88 200th anniversary of the Augsburg Confession. Medal by J.C. Hedlinger. 1730. AR. George III Swedish Medals 47.

III.3.89 Erasmus. Medal by H. Frei. 1907. AE. 1934-10-27-4. Presented by the artist.

The Dassiers

Jean Dassier (1676-1763), Switzerland's most celebrated medallist, was born in Geneva and trained under his father Domaine Dassier, chief-engraver at the Geneva mint, and in Paris. From 1731 he lived and worked in Britain. Some of his larger medals are masterpieces of die-engraving, but his fame rests more on the various series of medals he executed from the 1720s on. In some of these he was helped by his son Jacques Antoine Dassier (1715-1759), who also produced a series of famous Englishmen of his own time, which included the founder of the British Museum, Sir Hans Sloane. He later worked at the mint of St. Petersburg in Russia.

Jean Dassier

III.3.90 Clovis. From the series of French monarchs. AE. George III French Medals 835.

III.3.91 Archbishop William Wake. Dedicatory medal from the series of reformers, 1725. AR. George III Illustrious Persons 1151.

III.3.92 Luther. From the series of reformers. AE, AR. George III Illustrious Reformers AR 9.

III.3.93 Calvin. From the series of reformers. AE. 1927-7-22-40. Presented by Mr. T.H.B. Graham.

III.3.94 Beza. From the series of reformers. AE. George III Illustrious Reformers AE 24.

III.3.95 Wycliffe. From the series of reformers. AE. George III Illustrious Reformers AE 3.

III.3.96 Knox. From the series of reformers. AR. M 6882.

III.3.97 Death of George I. 1727. AR, AE. George III English Medals 266. M 8239.

III.3.98

*III.3.98 William I. From the series of British monarchs. Damascened AE, AE. George III English Medals Dassier 1. 1865-3-24-1581. Presented by the Bank of England.

III.3.99 Oliver Cromwell. From the series of British monarchs. AR. George III British Medals 204.

III.3.100

*III.3.100 George II. Dedicatory medal from the series of British monarchs, 1731. AR. George III English Medals of Dassier 32.

III.3.101 Shakespeare. AR, AE. 1878-9-1-1. George III Illustrious Persons 1022.

III.3.102 Newton. AE. George III Illustrious Persons 733.

III.3.103 Molière. From the series of Illustrious French men. AE. George III French Medals 932.

III.3.104 Mazarin. From the series of Illustrious French men. AE. George III French Medals 920.

III.3.105 Romulus. From the ancient Roman series. AR. M 4515.

III.3.106 Rape of the Sabine women. From the ancient Roman series. AR. M 4516.

III.3.107 Louis the Strong. 1734. AR, AE. 1863-11-14-46. Presented by Count J.F.W. de Salis. George III Illustrious Persons 388.

*III.3.108 Republic of Geneva. 1749. AE. Townshend, p.226,4.

III.3.109 Republic of Berne. AR. Townshend, p.89, 16. M 1982.

III.3.110 J.F. Osterwald. 1740. M 8449.

Jacques Antoine Dassier

III.3.111 Alexander Pope. 1741. AE. George III Illustrious Persons 792.

III.3.112 Robert Walpole. 1744. AE. M 8483.

*III.3.113 Edmund Halley. 1744. AE. M8491.

*III.3.114 Hans Sloane. 1744. AE. M 8490. 1966-4-3-642. Presented by Mr. W.E. Watts.

III.3.113

III.3.115 Dissolution of the Lausanne Literary Society. 1748. AR. Townshend, p.276.

III.3.116 State of England. 1750. AE. M 8599. George III English Medals 196.

III.3.117 Foundation of the Moscow Academy. 1754. AR. M 0843.

The Helvetic Republic

With the Napoleonic invasion and the ensuing proclamation of the Helvetic Republic on 12 April 1798, Switzerland was transformed into a centralised state. The coinage was also transformed, with the replacement of local coinage by a unified issue. The Treaty of Lunéville of 1802 paved the way for the Act of Mediation which provided Switzerland with a new constitution.

III.3.118 Geneva. Génévoise. 1794. AR. Townshend, p.214,217. 1947-6-7-27. Presented by the family of Dr. S. Fairbairn.

III.3.119 Geneva. Mi-Décime. 1794. AR. Townshend, p. 215, 221. Townshend, p.215, 221A.

III.3.120 Geneva. 5 Centimes. 1799/1801. AE. Townshend, p.218, 240. Townshend, p.218, 241.

III.3.121 First year of the Helvetic Republic. Medal. 1798. AE. 1947-6-7-647. Presented by the family of Dr. S. Fairbairn.

III.3.122

*III.3.122 Helvetic Republic. 32 Francs. 1800. AV. Townshend, p.576,1. 1855-1-26-4.

III.3.123 Helvetic Republic. 40 Batzen. 1798. AR. Townshend, p.577,5. 1860-5-1-4. Presented by Count J.F.W. de Salis.

III.3.124 Helvetic Republic. 1 Rappen. 1800. Billon. Townshend, p.579,23. Townshend, p.579,24.

III.3.125 Sarine and Broye. 42 Kreuzer. 1798. AR. Townshend, p.328,2. Townshend, p. 328, 3.

III.3.126 Neuchâtel. Half Ecu. 1799. AR. Townshend, p. 328,2. Townshend, p. 328,3.

III.3.127 Treaty of Lunéville. Medal by C.A. Mercié. 1802. Bronzed lead. 1947-6-7-694. Presented by the family of Dr. S. Fairbairn.

The Cantons Restored

With the Act of Mediation, sovereignty was restored to the cantons, but full independence from France was not achieved until the defeat of Napoleon in 1815. Along with the restoration of the cantons came

the reinstatement of cantonal minting rights, although a unified denominational system was retained. A series of conferences in the 1830s failed to bring about closer monetary co-operation. The principality of Neuchâtel was ruled by Napoleon's general Alexandre Berthier from 1806 to 1814, when it reverted to Prussia.

III.3.128 Lucerne. 20 Franks. 1807. AV. Townshend, p.279,9. 1861-12-3-12.

III.3.129 Fribourg. 4 Francs. 1813. AR. Townshend, p. 143,71.

III.3.130 Ticino. 4 Franchi. 1814. AR. Townshend, p.417,1.

III.3.131 Vaud. 10 Batzen. 1804. AR.Townshend, p.464,12.

III.3.132 Solothurn. Frank. 1812. AR. Townshend, p.394,50.

III.3.133 Glarus. 45 Rappen. 1806/7. Billon. Townshend, p.237,2. Townshend, p.237,3.

III.3.134 Appenzell. Batzen. 1808. Billon. Townshend, p.11,6. Townshend, p. 11,7.

III.3.135 Thurgau. Batzen. 1809. Billon. Townshend, p.425,4.

III.3.136 St. Gallen. Batzen. 1815. Billon. Townshend, p.176,8.

*III.3.137 Neuchâtel. 2 Francs. 1814. AR. Townshend, p.320,69. 1859-6-1-28.

III.3.137

III.3.138 Neuchâtel restored to Frederick-William III of Prussia. Medal by H.F. Brandt. 1814. AE. Townshend, p.324,5.

III.3.139 Berne. French écus. 1770/93, countermarked. AE. AR. Townshend, p.84,257. 1947-6-7-29. Presented by the family of Dr. S. Fairbairn.

III.3.140 Aargau. 10 Batzen. 1818. AR. Townshend, p.2,5. 1841-12-22-635.

*III.3.141 Graubünden. 10 Batzen. 1825. AR. Townshend, p.243,4. 1841- 12-22-786.

III.3.141

III.3.142 Berne. Batzen. 1826. Billon. 1860-5-1-185. Presented by Count J.F.W. de Salis. Townshend, p.75,166.

III.3.143 Geneva. 10 Francs. 1848. Townshend, p.187,15. 1849-9-24-2.

1848 and Stability

A number of medals record the conflicts of the 1840s which were resolved by the adoption of the federal constitution of 1848. Although the cantons retained sovereignty, the federal authorities moved to unify communications and the economy and a single national currency was introduced in 1850. The country's subsequent stability has been reflected in its coinage which has remained remarkably unchanged to this day. Few alterations have been made to the designs, the most significant development being the move from precious to base metals.

III.3.144 Expulsion of the Jesuits from Vaud. Medal. 1845. AR. Townshend, p.475,1. Townshend, p.475,2.

III.3.145 Defeat of the *Sonderbund* by General Dufour. Medal by J. Sieber. 1847. AE. Townshend, p.597,24.

*III.3.146 Republic of Neuchâtel secured. Medal by S. Mognetti. 1856. AE. Townshend, p.325,7.

*III.3.147 4 Francs proof by A. Bovy. 1855. AR, AE. 1935-4-1-13287. T.B. Clarke-Thornhill bequest. Townshend, p.586,1.

III.3.147

III.3.148 20 Centimes proof. 1855. AE. Townshend, p.586,2.

III.3.149 10 Centimes proof. 1850. AE. Townshend, p.586,3.

III.3.150 2 Francs proof by A. Bovy. 1860. AR. Townshend, p.583,5. Townshend, p.583,6.

III.3.151 20 Francs. 1871. AV. 1935-4-13271. T.B. Clarke-Thornhill bequest.

III.3.152 20 Francs. 1873. AV. 1935-4-1-13272. T.B. Clarke-Thornhill bequest.

III.3.153 20 Francs. 1883/94. AV. 1935-4-1-13273. T.B. Clarke-Thornhill bequest. 1913-12-4-121. Lady Ramsay bequest.

III.3.154 20 Francs. 1901/2. AV. 1903-7-5-1. Presented by Mr. H.A. Grueber. 1909-2-2-137. Presented by Mrs. M.E. Thornton.

III.3.155 5 Francs. 1850. Townshend, p.582,1. 1851-7-8-2.

III.3.156 5 Francs. 1889/94. AR. 1891-10-6-1. Presented by Mr. S. Smith. 1913-12-4-119. Lady Ramsay bequest.

III.3.157 5 Francs. 1922. AR. 1923-8-4-1. Presented by Mr. O.W. Dalton. 1940-10-2-4. Presented by Mrs. H. Thompson.

III.3.158 5 Francs. 1931. AR. 1964-1-12-1. Presented by Mr. R.A.G. Carson.

III.3.159 2 Francs. 1850. AR. 1852-2-27-2. Townshend, p.582,3.

III.3.160 2 Francs. 1874. AR. 1875-10-2-6.

III.3.161 2 Francs. 1978. Cupro-nickel. 1985-1-18-2. Presented by Mr. M.P. Jones.

III.3.162 20 Centimes. 1850. Billon. 1852-1-6-1. Presented by the Earl of Enniskillen. Townshend, p. 584,13.

*III.3.163 20 Centimes. 1881. Nickel. C4116.

III.3.163   *III.3.164*

*III.3.164 20 Centimes. 1981. Cupro-nickel. 1985-1-18-3. Presented by Mr. M.P. Jones.

III.3.165 2 Centimes. 1850. AE. Townshend, p.585,24. 1851-7-8-5.

III.3.166 2 Centimes. 1942. Zinc. 1961-4-10-12. Presented by Mr. G.A. Morris.

III.3.167 2 Centimes. 1948/51. AE. 1957-4-1-1. Presented by Mr. L. Fisher. 1957-9-1-2. Presented by Mr. J. Maitland.

III.3.168 50th anniversary of the Republic of Neuchâtel. Medal by Huguenin Frères. 1898. AE. 1947-6-7-513. Presented by the family of Dr. S. Fairbairn.

Arms and Neutrality

Switzerland's policy of neutrality, espoused after her defeat at the hands of the French at the battle of Marignano (1515), has taken different forms at different times. For much of the period between Marignano and Napoleon's invasion, it was impaired by an unequal alliance with France, renewed from 1521 by successive treaties, some of which were commemorated by medals. The Treaty of Westphalia guaranteed Swiss independence, but the country's neutrality was not recognised internationally until the Congress of Vienna (1815). In order to preserve its independence and neutrality in the 19th and 20th centuries, Switzerland has put much emphasis on military preparedness. Shooting festivals are an important part of this strategy and have led to the production of large numbers of medals. The official nature of these festivals is underlined by the coinage produced to commemorate them.

*III.3.169 Franco-Swiss alliance of 1663. Medal by J. Mauger. From the series of medals of the reign of Louis XIV, 1702. AR. George III French Medals 478.

III.3.170 Franco-Swiss alliance of 1777. Medal by J. Schwendimann. 1777. AR. Townshend, p. 413,4.

III.3.171 Peace of Westphalia celebrated in Basle. Medal by F. Fechter. 1648. AR. M1962.

III.3.172 Congress of Vienna of 1815. Medal by A.J. Depaulis. From Mudie's British National Medals, 1820. AE. 1913-12-4-99. Lady Ramsay bequest.

*III.3.173 Swiss neutrality during Franco-Prussian War. Medal of General Hans Herzog by C. Richard. 1871. AR. 1934-6-5-1. Presented by Mrs. J. Wyler.

III.3.174 International Peace Conference, Geneva. Medal. 1867. AE. M1974.

III.3.175 Foundation of the Red Cross. Medal. 1870. AE. 1906-11-3-1539. Presented by Dr. F. Parkes Weber.

III.3.176 First World War mobilisation. Medal by Huguenin Frères, 1919. AE. 1979-5-17-127. Presented by Prof. and Mrs. J. Hull Grundy.

III.3.177 Officers' shooting festival, Langenthal. Medal by A. Bovy. 1827. AE. Townshend, p.589,5.

*III.3.178 Federal shooting festival, Berne. 5 Francs. 1857. AR. 1935-4-1-13303. T.B. Clarke-Thornhill bequest.

III.3.178

III.3.179 Federal shooting festival, Stanz, Unterwalden. Medal by S. Drentwett. 1861. White metal. Townshend, p.436,1.

III.3.180 Federal shooting festival, St. Gallen. 5 Francs. 1874. AR. 1935-4-1-13127. T.B. Clarke-Thornhill bequest.

III.3.181 Zurich cantonal shooting festival, Winterthur. Medal by H. Wildermuth and H. Bovy. 1891. AR. 1981-8-2-32.

III.3.182 West Swiss shooting festival, Biel. Medal by R. Lanz and F. Homberg. 1893. AR. 1981-8-2-32.

III.3.183 Unterwalden cantonal shooting festival, Ennetmoos. Medal by E. Zimmermann. 1898. AR. 1981-8-2-31.

*III.3.184 3rd centenary of the Escalade, Geneva. Medal by H. Bovy. 1902. AR. 1978-7-12-45. Presented by Prof. and Mrs. J. Hull Grundy.

III.3.185 Federal shooting festival, Biel. Medal by Huguenin Frères. 1958. AR. 1962-11-25-2. Presented by Messrs Spink.

III.3.184

Paper Money

Switzerland was late in centralising its banking system. The cantonal structure impeded mergers between the country's banks, and also led to resistance to the creation of a national bank. Only in 1907 was the Swiss National Bank established, with a substantial proportion of its shares reserved for the cantons, and in 1910 it obtained a monopoly on the issuing of banknotes. The designs of the country's banknotes have, like those of its coins, remained remarkably static, with only three new sets of designs since 1910.

III.3.186   1000 Francs. 1923. 1984-6-5-424.

*III.3.187 500 Francs. 1923. 1984-6-5-425.

III.3.188   100 francs. 1920/45. 1984-6-5-420. 1984-6-5-434.

III.3.189   50 Francs. 1924. 1984-6-5-427.

III.3.190   20 Francs. 1939. 1984-6-5-430.

III.3.191   5 Francs. 1921. 1984-6-5-421.

III.3.192   1000 Francs. 1954. On indefinite loan from the Chartered Institute of Bankers.

III.3.193   500 Francs. 1961. On indefinite loan from the Chartered Institute of Bankers.

III.3.194   100 Francs. 1956. On indefinite loan from the Chartered Institute of Bankers.

III.3.195   20 Francs. 1955. On indefinite loan from the Chartered Institute of Bankers.

The Modern Swiss Medal

A number of 19th and 20th century Swiss medallists have gained international reputations. The medals made by members of the Bovy family of Geneva are fine examples of 19th century classicism, whilst those of Charles Töpffer show that the contemporaneous revival of the cast portrait medal was felt also in Switzerland. Hans Frei's medals and plaquettes place him amongst the foremost practitioners of the art nouveau style in Europe. Switzerland's commitment to the contemporary medal is demonstrated by its regular participation in the exhibitions of the Fédération Internationale de la Médaille (FIDEM).

III.3.196   James Fazy. Medal by A. Bovy. 1855. AE. Townshend, p.231,18.

III.3.197   Antoine Bovy. Medal by H. Bovy. 1864. AE. 1906-11-3-1738. Presented by Dr. F. Parkes Weber.

III.3.198   Jean-Jacques Rousseau. Medal by C.J. Richard. 1878. AR. 1879- 10-1-1.

III.3.199   Self portrait. Medal by C. Töpffer. 1878. AE. 1977-4-12-6.

III.3.200   Arnold Böcklin. Medal by H. Sandreuther. 1897. AE. 1906-11-3- 1586. Presented by Dr. F. Parkes Weber.

III.3.201   J.H. Pestalozzi. Medal by H. Frei. 1895. AE. 1906-11-3-1670. Presented by Dr. F. Parkes Weber.

III.3.202 Glorious Basle. Medal of Hans Holbein by Hans Frei. 1897. AR. 1934-10-27-1. Presented by the artist.

III.3.203 The Swiss National Museum, Zurich. Medal by Hans Frei. 1898. AR, AE. 1906-11-3-1538. Presented by Dr. F. Parkes Weber. 1899-4-8-1. Presented by Mr. C.H. Read.

*III.3.204 Basle festival. Medal by Hans Frei. 1901. AE. 1965-4-6-1. Presented anonymously.

III.3.205 Alsace Shepherd Dog Society. Medal by Huguenin. Early 20th century. AR. 1978-7-12-44. Presented by Prof. and Mrs. J. Hull Grundy.

III.3.206 Swiss Swimming Championships, Fribourg. Medal by Huguenin, 1932. AE. 1979-5-17-91. Presented by Prof. and Mrs. J. Hull Grundy.

III.3.207 Indian Women II. Medal by C. Seth-Höfner. 1970s. AE. 1978-12-13-4.

Select Bibliography

Reginald Stuart Poole, *A Descriptive catalogue of the Swiss coins in the South Kensington Museum bequeathed by the Reverend Chauncy Hare Townshend* (London: Science and Art Department, 1878). [Referred to above as 'Townshend'].

Jean-Paul Divo and Edwin Tobler, *Die Münzen der Schweiz im 17. Jahrhundert; 18 Jahrhundert; 19 und 20. Jahrhundert* (Zurich: Bank Leu AG, 1987; 1974; 1967).

F.X. Weissenrieder, *100 Jahre schweizerisches Münzwesen 1850-1950* (Berne: Eidg. Münzstätte, 1950).

Urs Graf, *Swiss paper money 1881-1968* (Münster: Numismatischer Verlag H. Dombrowski, 1970).

T.R. Fehrenbach, *The Swiss banks* (New York: McGraw-Hill, 1966).

E. Hahn, *Jakob Stampfer* (Zurich: Beer, 1915).

Jean L. Martin, *Médailles suisses* (Lausanne, 1979; 1986).

Schweizer Medaillen aus altem Privatbesitz. Sale catalogue with introduction by Dietrich W.H. Schwarz (Zurich: Bank Leu AG, 1989).

Delbert Ray Krause, *Swiss shooting talers and medals* (Racine, Wisconsin, 1965).
Jean L. Martin, *Les Médailles de tir suisses* (Lausanne, 1972).

III.3.204

III.4 STAMPS

The early imperforate stamps of Switzerland

Switzerland's first postage stamps were issued by the canton of Zurich on 1st March 1843. The 4 and 6 rappen values were the first to be issued by a postal administration after the trail-blazing appearance in Great Britain, three years earlier, of the penny black and two penny blue. The 4 rappen pre-paid local postage, while the 6 rappen covered postage of greater distances within the canton.

The Alpenpost *circa* 1900. *maps* 197.d.19

Geneva followed Zurich's lead on 30th September 1843 when it issued a two-part stamp known as the 'Double Geneva'. It comprised two 5 centimes values, each valid for local postage, linked at the top by a framed '10 [PORT CANTONAL] CENT' panel indicating that if used together the stamps pre-paid postage further afield within the canton. Unlike the somewhat anonymous-looking Zurich issues, each stamp proudly displayed the distinctive cantonal arms. Further 5 centimes issues of a similar design were made in 1845 and 1847-8.

The canton of Basle-Town (the other half of the canton had become Basel-Land in 1833) introduced 2½ rappen stamps showing a dove surmounted by the crozier of Basle on 1st July 1845. The same principal applied as in Zurich and Geneva: the more stamps that were used, the further the letter was pre-paid. One 2½ rappen stamp pre-paid a local letter, two pre-paid a letter between the town and the suburbs or between the other communes of the canton. The 'Basle Dove', as it is known, was the first stamp to be printed in more than one colour, being in carmine, black and blue. It was also the first to be embossed.

The federal constitution of 12th September 1848 transferred the operation of the postal service from the cantons to the new central government based in Berne. This change did not take immediate effect, however, and while a country-wide Post Office was being established between 1849 and the first half of 1850 Geneva and Zurich continued to issue stamps. All the stamps of this transitional period include the national emblem of the federal cross. Several also featured an early form of the postal horn which was eventually to become the symbol of the Swiss postal service. Geneva issued a 4 centimes in October 1849 and a 5 centimes on 22 January 1850 followed by a 5 centimes of a different design in August 1850. Zurich issued a 2½ rappen stamp in March 1850.

Upon the establishment of the national, as opposed to cantonal, Post Office, the postal rates were fixed on 5th April 1850 as 2½ rappen for letters up to 2 loths (1 ounce) inclusive, 5 rappen for packets from 2 to 4 loths (1 to 2 ounces) and 10 rappen for 4 to 8 loths (2 to 4 ounces), Accordingly 2½ rappen federal issues appeared in May 1850, followed by 5 rappen and 10 rappen values in the October of the same year. The 2½ rappen appeared in two forms inscribed 'ORTS POST' and 'POSTE LOCALE' for the German and French-speaking parts of the country, but all incorporated the federal cross, either framed or unframed, some of which are rare.

From 1854 to 1862 a new issue of stamps appeared showing the allegorical figure of Switzerland, Helvetia, seated full face. Values between 5 and 40 rappen appeared with this design on a variety of types of paper with silk threads. These were the last of the early stamps and the next issue of 1862-7 were the first to be perforated.

Cantonal Administrations

III.4.1   Zurich 1843 horizontal red lined 4 r. black: a horizontal strip of five showing the five types, unused.

III.4.2 Zurich 1843 horizontal red lines, 6 r. black: a horizontal strip of seven including the five types, unused.

III.4.3 Geneva 1843 5 + 5 c. black on yellow-green, unused: the 'Double Geneva'.

III.4.4 Geneva 1845 5 c. black on yellow-green, used on piece.

III.4.5 Geneva 1847-8 5 c. black on yellow-green, an unused horizontal pair.

III.4.6 Geneva 1849 5 c. yellow-green, used on 1850 entire.

III.4.7 Basle 1845 2½ r. a proof in vermilion and green: the 'Basle Dove'.

III.4.8 Basle 1845 2½ r. carmine, black and blue, an unused vertical pair from bottom of sheet.

III.4.8

Transitional Administration

III.4.9 Geneva 1849 4 c. black and red, used on 1850 part entire.

III.4.10 Geneva 1850 (August) 5 c. black and red, used on 1850 part entire.

III.4.11 Zurich 1850 2½ black and red, a used horizontal pair.

Federal Administration

III.4.12 1850 (May) inscribed 'ORTS POST' 2½ r. black and red. Central cross without frame, used.

III.4.13 1850 (May) inscribed 'POSTE LOCALE' 2½ r., black on red. Central cross without frame, used.

III.4.14 1850 (1st October) 5 r. black and blue. Central cross with black frame, unused.

III.4.15 1850 (1st October) 10 r. black and orange-yellow. Central cross with black frame, unused.

III.4.16 1854-62 5 r. brown, 10 r. blue, 15 r. rose, 20 r. orange, 40 r. green.

III.4.17 Telegraph Stamps: 1868-9 25 c. grey and carmine, 50 c. blue carmine, 1 fr. green and carmine, 3 fr. gold and carmine, 20 fr. pink and carmine.

All the above are from the Tapling Collection.

Modern stamps 1900-1987

Modern Swiss issues are distinguished by the charity, 'Pro Juventute' issues which have been appearing since 1913. These are sold at a premium, with the amounts additional to the face value being donated to a children's charity.

All unused.

III.4.18 1900 25th anniversary of the Universal Postal Union, set.

III.4.19 1919-20 Airmail 30 c and 50 c. in blocks of four.

III.4.20 1919 Peace celebration. 15 c. yellow and violet.

III.4.21 1928 Pro Juventute 30 c. blue and scarlet commemorating centennial of birth of Henri Dunant, founder of the Red Cross.

III.4.21

III.4.28

III.4.22   1932 International Disarmament Conference. 1 fr. grey and blue.

III.4.23   1937 Pro Juventute 5 c. + 5 c. blue green with portrait of General Guillaume-Henri Dufour, victor of the *Sonderbund* War and cartographer.

III.4.23

III.4.24   1940 National Fete and Red Cross Fund, set. The celebration on the meadow at Rütli on Switzerland's national day, 1st August, was a defiant assertion of independence shortly after the German conquest of France and Italy's entry into the Second World War. It marked the ascendancy of General Henri Guisan over would-be appeasers in the government and administration.

III.4.25   1940 Pro Juventute 5 c. + 5 c. green, with portrait of Johann Caspar Lavater, philosopher and political theorist.

III.4.26   1941-8 Airmail, 70 c. violet on salmon. The Maggia delta, Lago Maggiore, can be seen below the plane.

III.4.27   1941 National Fete and 650th anniversary of the foundation of the Swiss Confederation. 10 c + 10 c. blue, scarlet and yellow.

III.4.28   1942 Salvage campaign, 10 c. brown, inscribed in Italian.

III.4.29   1945 Peace, set.

III.4.30   1947 Pro Juventute 5 c. + 5 c. green.

III.4.31   1948 Fifth Winter Olympic Games at St. Moritz, set.

III.4.32   1957 Pro Juventute 5 c. + 5 c. claret with the portrait of Leonhard Euler, mathematician.

III.4.33   1967 Publicity Issue 40 c. multicoloured: European Free Trade Association [of which Switzerland is a member].

III.4.34   1978 Jura, 23rd canton of the Federation. 40 c. bright scarlet, black and yellow-ochre with arms of Jura and Switzerland.

III.4.35   1979 Publicity Issue 40 c. multicoloured. 50th Federal Riflemen's Festival, Lucerne: a recent manifestation of an ancient tradition.

III.4.36   1980 Publicity Issue 80 c. commemorating opening of St. Gotthard Road Tunnel.

III.4.37   1982 Europa 40 c. and 60 c.: swearing Oath of Eternal Fealty and Treaty of 1291 founding Swiss Confederation.

III.4.38   1987 Tourism 40 c.

Issues of international organisations situated in Switzerland

III.4.39   League of Nations: 1938 30 c. blue and pale blue overprinted SPECIMEN in red.

III.4.40   International Labour Office 1923-44 10 fr. dull purple.

III.4.41   International Education Office 1950 5 c. orange.

III.4.42   World Health Organisation: 1957-60 30 c. orange.

III.4.43   International Telecommunications Union 1958-60 40 c. blue.

III.4.44   United Nations 1960 15th anniversary of United Nations 5 fr. greenish blue.

Nos. 10.18-44 are from the Universal Postal Union Collection.